The Rise of Female Leaders in Egypt

Juhainah Bilqees

ABSTRACT

The purpose of this is to conduct a qualitative phenomenological study with the intention to explain, explore, and determine the factors that lead to the emergence of women as leaders in Egypt. Accomplishing this investigation required the assessment of how participants perceive a condition through experience and consciousness and how events appear from a first-person point of view. The purposefully selected participants were women in leadership roles in both the public and private sectors. Ten women were interviewed two times each over six months. The study attempts to shed light on the factors that contribute to women in Egypt obtaining leadership positions. This study investigated the factors that contribute to the lack of women acquiring positions of management, guidance, and leadership -- positions usually dominated by men in Egypt by asking: (a) What are the perceived factors that contribute to the lack of women acquiring positions of management, guidance, and leadership? and (b) What are the perceived positions of leadership women occupy the most? Information was collected from the interviewee using the guide approach to provide a focus for the researcher and participants. This approach permitted a certain amount of autonomy and flexibility to acquire the appropriate information from the interviewee. The interviews consisted of presenting open-ended questions allowing women to reflect on how they were successful in obtaining these leadership positions. The study revealed four pertinent themes: (a) family influence, (b) leadership position, (c) family obligations, and (d) level of education.

TABLE OF CONTENTS

Chapter 1

Introduction

The emergence of women leaders in Egypt has begun in force, fuelled by the revolutions, uprisings, and the current condition of the country. In a culture in which men commonly dominate, in the last 10 years, the transformation of women's positions in society has made significant changes (Guenena, n.d.). The demonstrations and protests leading to the end of an era with the authoritarian administration of President Hosni Mubarak, Egyptian women are emerging as leaders and liberators (King, 2011). Women in the Muslim world envy the position Egyptian women have in their societies. They attend university, work outside the home, dress in secular styles, and drive automobiles (Siddiqi, 2006). Perhaps in consequence, recently more women in the Middle East have shed the conservative value system and joined educated, professional communities. Unfortunately, discrimination, prejudice, domestic violence, restricted legal rights, lack of representation in leadership positions, and overall inequity continue (King, 2011). Considering the positive atmosphere women are experiencing, sexual harassment is still an issue. For a brief period during the demonstrations, women did not have to contend with the sexual harassment that occurs frequently to both Egyptian and foreign women. However, it is still an endemic problem (Marshall, 2011).

The revolution in Cairo and the protests in Tahrir Square not only ousted Egypt's former president Hosni Mubarak, but also provided an opportunity for the country's women to fight for equal rights (Morgan, 2011). Women are continuing to work and organize to ensure they too will have a voice and remain equal cohorts in the transition of political power. Religion and cultural traditions dictate a set of rules pertaining to appropriate norms and behaviors expected of women in the Middle East (Thomas, 2011). Nevertheless, the revolution and new movements in Egypt see women emerging and engaging in leadership roles. Prior to the uprisings in Egypt, women were less likely to occupy positions of authority, management positions, and supervisory roles. Thomas (2011) explains that although it only took a few weeks to overthrow the regime, it will take a much longer time to transform the traditions that prefer authoritarian leadership, as it is the only leadership Egypt has seen in the last 40 years.

The problem investigated focused on women in Egypt as leaders and questioned why there are fewer women leaders than men leaders, positions that the male dominated society now deems appropriate and acceptable to women of this culture. Women who show initiative may be swift to move into leadership positions, and because they have achieved the goals they have set for themselves, they may be able to assist other women. Women as role models in Egypt can provide valuable information to other women and girls who aspire to lead.

Background of the Problem

Leadership roles for women vary from country to country and culture to culture. The roles of women in Egypt derive from what men or society deems acceptable, generally in the areas of culture, family, women's issues, marriage, and education (Abu-Lughod, 2006). Exceptions, such as family ties and succession, pressure from social groups, pressure to appease the West, and appointed positions, play an integral part in the procurement of these positions occupied by women (Youssef, 2002). To change the perception that other cultures have of the Egypt as oppressive to the female race (Abu-Lughod, 2006), women are attempting to become more active in the attainment of leadership positions. Unfortunately, women throughout Egypt are sometimes deemed second-class citizens, denied full legal identities by exclusion from the rights, privileges, and security entitled to individuals of society (Harik & Marsston, 2003).

Feminism as a movement is believed to have first emerged in Egypt sometime between 1923 and 1939. Hoda Shaarawi was one of the first women's rights activists and began the movement as the first woman to take off her veil in public. This radical move was the beginning of women as feminists and Shaarawi's establishment of the Egyptian Feminist Union (EFU). The EFU campaigned for better health care, educational opportunities, and raising of the marriage age to 16 for women (Aguirre, Cavanaugh, & Sabbagh, 2011). These developments all helped improve the lives of Egyptian women (Tyldesley, 1994). Education, laws, and social welfare for women were concerns of the EFU (Tyldesley, 1994).

Ancient Egyptian history reveals that the position women played in Egyptian society was equal to men. Female gods played an important position in religion and were equal to male gods in their importance and influence (Fletcher, 2011). Mutt, Isis, and Hathor reigned over many aspects of ancient Egyptian life as rulers, landowners, and other high status positions position of women in Pharaonic society. Sobekneferu, Hatshepsut, and Cleopatra VII were female pharaohs who were queens. Their regents, Meritneith and Ahmose-Nefertari occupied high-status positions as God's Wife of Amun (*History of women in Egyptian life*, n.d.).

Women's feminism initially began the entry into society as a justifiable and essential element for a nationalist power (Trofin & Tomescu, 2010). The beginning of the first two centuries perceived a guarded social feminism. The following three decades continued to see feminism grow into a powerful and influential political movement (Trofin & Tomescu, 2010). The Revolution in 1952 silenced feminism and the state assumed the role of determining nationals' rights inside the context of Arab socialism (Badran, 2011). In the 1970s there was another resurgence of the feminist movement. In the 1980s, feminism became a vivacious power as the public began to find many voices supporting the movement (Badran, 2011). The third wave of feminism emerged in the

1990s and people began to rethink feminism and how it may develop in the future (Badran, 2011).

Statement of the Problem

Today Egypt's women may go to school, attend university, have employment in the civil sector, vote, and run for political office. However, literacy rates in Egypt remains at 58% for women and they comprise only 23% of the workplace (Marshall, 2011). The laws in Egypt are tenuous (*The Economist*, 2011). For example, the constitution forbids sex discrimination, women inherit half the amount of men. Divorce laws are discriminatory, as well: men have only to appear before a civil servant to divorce their wives but women must suffer prolonged proceedings in court. In addition, a woman loses custody of her children if she remarries (*The Economist*, 2011).

President Mubarak and the old regime defended women's rights as a way of appearing to the West that they were concerned. They also defended women's right to stifle on their Islamist opponents (Marshall, 2011). Suzanne Mubarak also supported and defended women's rights. Laws permitting women to be judges and outlawing female genital mutilation are standing even now, but are now considered to foul because they are associated with the former regime (Marshall, 2011). Hoda Badran, from the Alliance for Arab Women indicates that these laws were not Suzanne Mubarak's. She provided her support for these laws in the end even though the Alliance was responsible for the actual work (King, 2011).

Egyptians are distrustful of the rhetoric used in women's rights, and considered the movement driven and imported from the West. The purpose of the revolution was to separate and rid Egypt of all the issues connected to the decades of Mubarak's rule, but advocates worry that the rights of women will not be as strong as they once were and will suffer (*The Economist*, 2011). Present literature investigates disparities of women's rights in the Arab world, advocates for the elimination of legal discrimination against women, and aids in obtaining their legal rights (Trofin,

& Tomescu, 2010).

In the past 10 years, the Egyptian government and political leaders have initiated reforms to deal with gender discrimination in laws and policies (Marshall, 2011). There are spaces available for women according to a system of quotas, a policy that has been in place since the mid-1980s. Approximately 12% of seats in Egypt's parliament are for women (King, 2011). In another effort to include women in politics, the 2009 parliament ratified a law allotting women 64 of the 518 seats in the People's Assembly (Marshall, 2011). The system of quotas was eradicated since the revolution, but women are divided on whether this should be a concern. The old regime and President Mubarak were ousted and anything relating to this group was dismissed. This included women who obtained positions by the quota system (*The Economist*, 2011). The standing of women in Egyptian politics has deteriorated significantly since the overthrow of Mubarak (King, 2011).

In the Middle East, it is necessary for women to assume roles of leadership in the public arena to promote gender equality. General Assembly President Ali Treki stated, "The Middle East is a vast, diverse region and the status of women varies significantly from one country to the other," (U.N. speaks up for Mideast women, 2007, para. 5). In some regions, women are still faced with discrimination on many fronts deeply rooted in the legal framework, educational system, and culture. Family laws vary from culture to culture and are subjected entirely too dissimilar social frameworks. Emphasis is placed on the importance of understanding the content of Islamic texts based on issues pertaining to this century (U.N. speaks up for Mideast women, 2007) .

In Egypt, the predominance of values steeped in tradition continues to dominate the belief systems of both men and women. Often they favor autocratic leadership. The lack of women leaders in politics, private and public sectors, and judiciary positions is common (Kamal, 2011).

Religious and cultural traditions dictate a set of rules pertaining to appropriate norms and behaviors (Thomas, 2011). Nevertheless, the revolution and new movements in Egypt are seeing women emerging and engaging in leadership roles. Prior to the uprisings in Egypt women were less likely to occupy positions of authority, management positions, and supervisory roles that led entire groups of people or organizations (Atwater, Wang, Smither, & Fleenor, 2009).

Study Procedure

In this study, women leaders were interviewed regarding their experiences in obtaining positions of authority, management, and supervision and then the study investigated these experiences. The purpose of this qualitative phenomenological study is to explore women's perceptions and lived experiences of emerging as leaders in Egypt. An open-ended questionnaire pertaining to successful women and their obtainment of leadership positions provided information for analysis. Research by scholars in the field who employ similar methods and designs assisted to garner information for this study. Women leaders and those striving to become leaders comprised the sample group for interviews. They were asked to reflect on women in Cairo, leadership positions, new issues, and courses of actions.

Women in Egypt today.

Women do not share the same privileges as men in Egypt. Discriminatory constitutions, biased mentalities, and unjust laws violate women's rights (Badran, 2011). Gender-based violence continues to be an obstacle for women in Egypt (Abu-Lughod, 2006). Women are not protected from spousal abuse and the laws to safeguard them are absent in most Middle Eastern countries. Honor killings and spousal rape still exist and are not against the law (Abu-Lughod, 2006). Egypt does not see many cases of this criminal behavior; however, it is becoming concerning because of the January 25 revolution (Thomas, 2011).

The patriarchal nature of the culture and the lack of legal literacy contribute to barriers that women face when trying to access justice systems (Badran, 2011). The emergence of women's rights in Egypt exists but traditional values endure (Harik & Marsston, 2003). To arrive at a viewpoint in line with modern practices and principles that other cultures embody, Egyptian men and women must change their thinking. The modern perspective contradicts the way men and women have understood their customs and culture their entire lives (Thomas, 2011).

Change in the Egypt is evident more than ever before. Prior to the January 25th revolution, women contributed their leadership skills and continue to be proactive in the cause of democracy. They act as role models and are agents of change in their cultural communities. The political upheaval in the Middle East recently has alerted attention to the region.

Research conducted by Kristof (2008) finds that women measure up to men, and even outshine them in agreement structuring and other specific skills beneficial to positions requiring leadership, guidance, and control. The integration of women into Egyptian society and their participation in the public sector and leadership roles this century has brought immense changes to the country (Guenena, n.d.).

There is a concerted effort to include women fully into all aspects of public life, though not without controversy. Stereotypes surface and contradictions from religious factions and conservatives versus those supporting secular liberalism still exist (Thomas, 2011). Guenena (n.d.) indicates that political factions are including women so they may appear supportive. This is done to legitimize their popularity.

Women have become a larger influence in the workforce; the cumulative contribution of women working in jobs that produce an income is increasing. The gender gap among those employed is decreasing (Youssef, 2002). During the 1980s and 1990s, the growth of the labor force was significantly higher for women than men for every region of the world except Africa and the Middle East (Youssef, 2002). In countries developed as industrialized nations, the female labor force is increasing, and this shift has decreased the number of children that women are having. (Youssef, 2002).

Expectations and social attitudes toward women continue to reinforce the perception people have of women in Egypt (Harik & Marsston, 2003). This study interviewed women leaders and activists in the forefront of the current uprisings who contributed their skills to the movements in Egypt. In addition, women who aspire to acquire leadership positions participated in interviews. This second group is included because it is assumed that a new generation will be fundamentally different from the generation it precedes. The young people participating in the planning of the revolutions offered a transformative example. The current group of young men and women leading the drastic changes occurring in Egypt provided this example.

Kamal (2011) explores the rise of women leaders in the Middle East and the differences between the past and the present. He indicates that there is a sign of equality and acceptance toward women accomplishing career goals and sharing responsibilities with men. There is a shift in the mentality of men and their traditional views pertaining to women. Kamal (2011) also states that although the Middle East has made advances in the treatment of women, there are still issues that need to be addressed and not all people and places will be able to accept women in positions previously dominated by men (Thomas, 2011).

Purpose and Significance of the Study

The purpose of the study was to explore women's perceptions and lived experiences of emerging as leaders in Egypt. The participation of women in the revolution and protest in Egypt brought about the emergence of women in leadership positions. These women had not only audacity but they sacrificed in ways equivalent to men in the uprisings. There are women running for office, activists, and other leaders materializing from this historic time in Egypt's history (Guenena, n.d). Laila Soueif is an example. A mathematics professor at American University of Cairo and mother of Alaa Abdel Fattah, she was one of the revolutionary bloggers and a "thorn in the backside of the military" (King, 2011, para. 5).

In December 2010, a street vendor in Tunisia, set himself on fire in a personal demonstration against the unfair treatment of his people by the Tunisian government (Pfeffer, 2011). Within weeks, widespread protests in support of his activities that resulted in his death on the streets resulted in the fall of the government. Anti-government protest in Egypt and Libya overthrew dictators after decades of ruling their countries and similar situations erupted from Syria to Yemen (Pfeffer, 2011).

The outcomes of the protests in these countries resulted in women joining the revolutionary fight and the transformation of the status of their countries (Sherwood, 2011). In Tahrir Square to Yemen, where women went to the streets and in defiance burned their veils, the risk and courage these women exhibited motivated women worldwide (Pfeffer, 2011). The Nobel Peace Prize was awarded to a young mother in Yemeni, thus making a profound and powerful statement of support internationally for her endeavors to improve women rights, democracy, and human rights in Yemen (Kamall, 2011).

Women in the Middle East experience struggles that are not unlike struggles women across the globe face as they try to rise to the top levels of their respective industries and careers; however, women in the Middle East face additional struggles (Aguirre, Cavanaugh, & Sabbagh, 2011). These women are blocked by "the cement ceiling," as one woman has put it (see Definition of Terms below) (Trofin & Tomescu, 2010). The culture has constructed an almost impenetrable atmosphere of cultural, social, and legal obstacles that hinder the ability for these women to experience upward mobility in their careers ("Building Gender Balanced Businesses", 2007). This study hoped to shed light on the process women have gone through to become leaders of their respective organizations, political and social groups, educational institutions, and other entrepreneurial pursuits. The aim was to determine how successful leaders have obtained this status and reached their goals.

Egypt is a complex country with many cultural characteristics that make the dynamics of a woman's place in society different from that in Western cultures (Marshall, 2011). Egyptian and Middle Eastern women have made strides concerning their rights, occupations, careers, education, and political aspirations. In the book, *Feminist, Islam, and nation: Gender and the making of modern Egypt,* Badran (2011) states that most accounts of the history of Egypt are written by men and can give a skewed and one-sided view. The author attempts to follow and trace the development of national sentiment by focusing on the rise of feminism in Egypt. Badran (2011), indicates that feminist consciousness is developed by more women becoming actively involved in political and social activities and organizations. Some individuals believe that men are the prototypical leaders and that women are not capable of balancing their family obligations and the management of organizations (Aguirre, Cavanaugh, & Sabbagh, 2011).

Research Questions

What are the implications from lived experiences Egyptian women face in their continuing roles of leadership in the post Arab Spring atmosphere?

1. What are the perceived factors that contribute to the lack of women acquiring positions of management, guidance, and leadership?

2.   What are the perceived positions of leadership women occupy the most?

More men than women are leaders, politicians, and activists in Egypt and fewer women have the opportunity to obtain these roles. The issues that influence the shortage of women acquiring positions of management, guidance, and leaders were explored. The question regarding how the positions were acquired was studied. Men dominate leadership and management positions in industries that drive the economy, such as technology, finance, manufacturing, and agriculture (Riggio, 2010). A majority of political leaders, Fortune 500 CEOs, and other managers are men. This is even true in the United States, a dominant force with the largest economy in the world (Riggio, 2010). By contrast, women generally are in charge of the household or other activities acceptable and appropriate to their culture (Badran, 2011).

Women leaders, scholars, and executives in Egypt were the population for this study. Using a phenomenological method, this study attempted to clarify precisely how women emerged as leaders by assessing the lived experience of participants in the study. The method examined phenomenology by looking at how participants perceive events through experience and consciousness from a first-person point of view (Groenewald, 2004). Qualitative methods gathered information and perceptions by means of participant observations, interviews, and by investigating the rise of Egyptian women as seen from participants in the study. Women participating in the uprisings were a part of a sample group for the purpose of this study. Additionally, women leaders were included in the study and their experiences of obtaining these positions were investigated.

Conceptual Framework

In the Middle East, women professionals or those aspiring to become professionals are faced with many challenges. Global competition makes it necessary for women to be involved in corporate, political, and civic workplaces (Moughari, 2010). Women in the Middle East face not only external but also internal pressures and to be successful a balance of these pressures is required, which is not an easy task (Orleans, 2004). Women across the globe face the some of the same difficulties when rising to the highest levels in the corporate and political arenas (Zahidi & Ibarra, 2010).

The additional obstacle of the "cement ceiling" previously mentioned, contributes to the difficulties Middle Eastern women face (DeAnne, Cavanaugh, & Sabbagh, 2011). Women who have managed to transcend the barriers and become successful have refused to accept the cultural expectations, attitudes, social norms, and legal dictums that dictate limitations on their lives (Metcalfe, 2008). Restrictions on traveling alone and other solitary activities hindered some women on their path to reach their potential. These women consistently insisted on improvements and exercised their capacity to step outside of their comfort zones in their personal and professional lives. In addition, they possessed tenacious confidence in their own competencies and ambitions to succeed in their ascent to the top.

Theory at Work.

Previous research indicates that in the last 10 years the number of women leaders in the Middle East increased. The Egyptian woman has continued to struggle with leadership roles, despite the achievements in education, political, and economic activity (Moughari, 2010). In the article "Women leaders wanted," Reem, writes, "Egyptian women will be extremely unique should they receive the appropriate learning, education and training to undertake the responsibilities and play the required roles of society" (Reem, 2009, para. 1). The theme that resonated with women interviewed was the burden of having to demonstrate not only an ability to deliver significant results but also to prove their value as an employee (Reem, 2009).

For a long time it has been difficult for Middle Eastern women to obtain positions in society and civil workplaces. In *The Economist* (2011), the Arab Human Development Report cites "the lack of women's rights as one of three factors, along with lack of political freedoms and poor education, that most hampered the region's progress (para. 2). Amid the loud calls for democracy in the early days of the uprisings, little was said specifically about women's rights" (Poulson, Smith, Hood, Arthur, & Bazemore, 2011, para. 4). The Egyptian revolution is seen as one of the more advanced revolutions, and a rewritten constitution represents hope to advance their liberation (*The Economist*, 2011).

Gender Role Theories.

Social learning theory interprets gender and role identity as behaviors learned from experiences and the environment. Gender behaviors that shape the way people conduct themselves and develop traits they may possess are often learned through observation (Poulson & Beck, 2006). The effect of gender on human diversity is an essential phenomenon that shapes almost every part of an individual's everyday life). Major theories offer explanations of gender development and the different aspects of these theories are important in understanding psychological, biological and sociological factors related to gender (Bussey & Bandura, 1999). Psychological theories lean toward intrapsychic processes, sociological theories emphasis sociostructural influences, and biologically oriented theories focus on biological roles in determining the development of gender-roles (Bussey & Bandura, 1999).

The social cognitive theory of gender-role development integrates psychological and sociostructural factors within an integrated theoretical structure and function (Bussey & Bandura, 1999). It identifies the construction of gender origins as a combination of experiences and the way these experiences operate together with motivation and self-regulatory mechanisms to influence behaviors of gender related behaviors (Bussey & Bandura, 1999).

Culture and gender share similar dynamics in the way they affect people's perceptions. In addition, they have invisible and visible factors that affect interpersonal and interrelational interactions of both individuals and groups (Bussey & Bandura, 1999). Cultural and ethnic tenets as well as gender-role beliefs and attitudes are learned through intrapsychic beliefs (Ayman & Korabik, 2010). Gender stereotypes are developed by social and physical appearances in the same way it is for people in different ethnic and cultural groups. According to Ayman & Korabik, (2010), the social structural perspective dictates that men leaders will attain outcomes different from women leaders under specific circumstances. This is particularly true in Egypt as men are the dominant gender in all aspects of their culture.

Leadership Theories.

Eagly and Carli's (2003) research on transactional and transformational leadership found that transformational leadership might be especially beneficial to women because of its androgynous qualities. Transformational leadership aims to motivate and inspire positive emotions among people and create a vision of the future (Avolio & Yammarino, 2008). A leader who has a vision and passion is capable of transforming a group or an individual toward the obtainment of a common goal (Eagly and Carli's, 2003). The transformational leader can instill trust within his or her subordinates creating a common vision. Transformational leaders are hands-on and involved in the transformation process. They strive to lead by example (Avolio & Yammarino, 2008). The extent that leaders are capable of transforming a situation is dependent on their influence over their subordinates. The leader uses charisma, individualized attention, and his or her inspiration to motivate followers to find new ways of working (Bass, 1990).

Definition of Terms

For the purpose of ensuring that the themes in this study are specifically defined, operational definitions will be utilized. Operational definitions chosen by a researcher can differ from one study to another (Cooper, 1982). A researcher may use the same label for a certain concept that may vary with other researchers and may use dissimilar operational definitions or abstraction levels (Cooper, 1982). A definition may include certain operations omitted by another researcher's definition or may encompass the other entirely (Herling, 2000).

The following presents the operational definitions for the purposes of this study:

Cement ceiling. Culture dictates that women face an almost impenetrable atmosphere of cultural, social, and legal obstacles that hinder the ability for these women to experience upward mobility in their careers (Building gender balanced businesses, 2007).

Dictator. A ruler who is essentially not constrained by laws, recognized opposition, constitutions, or political entity. An absolute ruler with whom no other person or group has any jurisdiction, especially tyrannical, ruler (Thomas, 2011).

Feminism. Justice, liberation, democracy, freedom, equality, rights, dignity are words that describe the new feminism. This concept was proclaimed during the revolution. Fundamental principles and human rights were restored to the lives of individuals, particularly women who were crushed during the Mubarak government. This new feminism could be stated as, "freedom, equality and justice for all." It proclaims its presence through courage, honesty, and action (Badran, 2011).

MENA Businesswomen's Network. The Middle Eastern North Africa Business Women's Network is an organization that represents women and offers a unified voice for women's rights and commerce and is committed to social progress around the world through economic development.

Pharaohs. A title given in modern discussions to the ancient Egyptian rulers of all time periods. The title meaning the "great house" originates in the term "pr-aa" and describes the royal palace. The New Kingdom used the title of Pharaoh for the king, specifically during the eighteenth dynasty (Fletcher, 2011).

Patriarchal. In Egypt, the social system and culture often dictates that the male is the primary authority figure central to the organization of social society. Specifically in patriarchal societies, fathers are the authority over women, children, and property. It entails female subordination and implies that men are the institution of rule and privilege (Petras, 2011).

Revolution. On Tuesday, January 25, 2011 the Egyptian people, after many days of protest and uprisings featuring acts of civil disobedience, series of demonstrations, labor strikes, and marches overthrew of the regime of Egyptian President Hosni Mubarak. Millions of protesters from all socio-economic and religious backgrounds banded together and made modern day history (King, 2011).

Seclusion. Cultural norms and traditions can result in a woman experiencing seclusion, prejudices, treatment, and restricted mobility. The restrictions women face in society are a part of the culture, tradition, and view that male supervision is essential and that women need protection in all aspects of their lives (Harik & Marsston, 2003).

Assumptions

The first assumption of the study was that the women who participate would not have preconceived notions as to the results of the study. The second assumption was that there would be consistencies in the participant's experiences with the experiences of other women in the same or similar positions and with women who wish to obtain positions of leadership. The third assumption was that the responses to the questions from the women who participated in the study would be honest and reliable, because they voluntarily agreed to participate in the study and their identity was anonymous.

Scope of the Study

The scope of the qualitative study included an in-depth analysis of the factors that lead to the emergence of women as leaders in Egypt and to explain, explore, and determine why there are fewer women leaders than men leaders, positions that the male dominated society now deems appropriate and acceptable to women of this culture. An investigation of the experiences of how women in positions of leadership obtained these positions gave rise to a better perception of the factors that are involved in securing high-level leadership positions for women in Egypt. The research design used the hermeneutic phenomenology approach for the analysis of the data.

The scope of the study limited the study to a size that was manageable and controllable to permit a methodical analysis of the data collected and completed in a timely manner (Groenewald, 2004). The scope applied to women in leadership positions within the geographic location of Egypt. It did not apply to women who were not currently in positions of leadership in their current occupations.

Interviews were conducted using the telephone and proved to be the most effective method for collecting data as the participants worked in different geographic locations and at different times of the day. The nature of the requirements of each participant's responsibilities and positions necessitated flexibility in both the location and time of the interviews. The interview questions were sent to the participants prior to the interviews in to ensure all questions were clear to all interviewees. The prescreening of the interview questions did not result in any modification of the questions in the interviews. The results of the study consisted in the development of themes, patterns, and explanations as to how women in leadership positions obtained these positions in a society dominated by a patriarchal culture norms.

Limitations

Egypt is currently experiencing a great deal of change politically, socially, culturally, religiously, and economically. One thing that has not changed is the cultural nuances that make Egypt a unique albeit challenging place for a foreigner to live. Egyptians are private people, and they socialize mainly with close friends and family. Bonds are strong among families and many work and live with their families often within the same property yet in their own residence. Egyptians' privacy will add a challenge to securing women for interviews. Most Egyptians are religious and their belief in a higher power plays a huge part in every aspect of their lives. The phrase, *In'shAllah* literally means "God willing," and this concept results in appointments missed, late arrivals, or not arriving. This can be frustrating and make people hard to pin down for an interview.

The limitations are those qualities of methodology or design that may have influenced or affected the explanation or understanding of the findings study. Limitations are the distinguishable restrictions that affect the generalizability and efficacy of findings and may be considered weaknesses of the study (Creswell, 2008). The research consisted of numerous limitations pertaining to women acquiring leadership positions in Egypt.

The first limitation of the study pertained to the size of the sample since the study included only 10 participants. Qualitative sampling confines the simplification of results to a general population (Creswell, 2008). Creswell's (2008) explanation for the limitation was it served to clarify the intention of qualitative investigation to develop of a comprehensive examination. Generalizability of a central phenomenon is not the study's intent.

A second limitation of the study was the visceral descriptions of the women's experiences in the study as expressed by the participants. The words of participants to express the account of their experiences are frequently used by qualitative researchers under study (Creswell, 2008). The nature of qualitative research approach is often subjective and may perhaps make findings individualistic and difficult to apply to circumstances beyond the research (Polit & Beck, 2006).

A third limitation pertains to the exactness of the process of coding the information acquired from the participant's interviews. Researcher bias is an intrinsic characteristic in the coding process, and personal feelings about a subject may influence a researcher and the coding process (Creswell, 2008). Additional biases may include the relevance of theories from other subjects that might seem applicable to the data in the process of coding (Foss & Waters, 2003). While researcher bias is understood as inevitable in qualitative research, the focus must be on the data and not on categorizing or relating it to familiar theories (Foss & Waters, 2003). Researcher bias was unavoidable and part of the qualitative research process. It is acknowledged and recorded through the entire study (Foss & Waters, 2003).

A fourth and final limitation was the data obtained in the interview. The interviewee's emotional, physical, and mental state often affects the interview. Vague responses due nervousness, personal bias, and anxiety can affect the interview data and are limitations of the interview process (Foss & Waters, 2003; Polit & Beck, 2006). The reactions between the interviewer and interviewee may affect the interview data as well (Polit & Beck).

Delimitations

The delimitations of the study are features that are constraints of the scope of a study as influenced by the purposeful exclusion and inclusion of choices formulated during development of the proposal (Creswell, 2008). Only women who were considered to be in positions of leadership in Egypt participated in the study. The outcomes of the study were contingent upon the answers to the interview questions from the participants in the study. For the collection of relevant data, the survey instrument consisted of open-ended interview questions designed with respect and sensitivity to the current situation in Cairo.

Summary

The struggle Middle Eastern women experience is similar to those women across the globe face when trying to rise to the top levels of their respective industries and careers (Trofin & Tomescu, 2010). However, women in the Middle East have additional struggles they face. These women are hindered by the "cement ceiling" (Building gender balanced businesses, 2007).

People in the western world often believe that Muslim women are oppressed by their religion, family, society, denied education, and other basic rights, and forced to cover themselves completely (Western, 2008). Muslim women, not unlike women all over the world, struggle with their rights and restrictive practices in education, equity, workforce participation, and family responsibilities (Siddiqi, 2006). Contrary to popular belief, these oppressive practices are part of local cultural traditions and do not come from Islam itself (Western, 2008). Some rights were not even enjoyed by Western women until the 19th century. For example, Islam gives women the right to retain their own assets, whereas until 1882, when they married, the property of women in England was given to husbands (Siddiqi, 2006). As well, Muslim women could stipulate provisions in their marriage contracts, such as the right to divorce should their husband take another wife (Global connections the Middle East, n.d.).

Women activists have brought about the emergence of transnational public spheres. Globalizing of cultures and societies are developing and becoming more interconnected; however, discrimination, disproportions, inequalities, and forms of governance still exist (Salih, 2010). Women around the world have unequal access to resources than their male counterparts. Limitations based on territoriality and national citizenship reinforce that women continue to experience imbalances around the globe and contribute to women's agendas. Women around the world continue to acquire empowering tools through feminist transnational networks but the dismantling of boundaries or weakening old hierarchies still exist (Salih, 2010).

This study intention was to bring to light the integration of women into Egyptian society and their participation in the public sector. It explored the implications of this century's effort to include fully women into all aspects of public life. The ability to make decisions and achieve personal goals, desires, or wishes is important in the transition women are making in the Middle East and Egypt. Cultural norms and traditions can result in a woman experiencing seclusion, prejudices, treatment, and restricted mobility (Siddiqi, 2006). The restrictions women face in society are a part of the culture, tradition, and the view that male supervision is essential and that women need protection in all aspects of their lives (Harik & Marsston, 2003).

For women to become more involved in the political and social process, an education is an important prerequisite. Education increases women's knowledge and their ability to advocate for not only women's issues but also current concerns. Women's lack of decision-making power and involvement in societal and public life has hindered their impact on discussions in regard to legal and political implications of gender issues (Salih, 2010).

Chapter 2

Review of Literature

Introduction

The intention of this qualitative phenomenological study was to delve into the perceptions and lived experiences of Egyptian women emerging as leaders in Egypt. For this investigative study, information was collected from 10 interviewees using the guide approach to provide a focus for the researcher and participants. The interviews consisted of presenting open-ended questions allowing women to reflect on how they were successful in obtaining these leadership positions. A range of scholarly peer-reviewed articles, books, internet websites, newspaper articles, and reports were investigated related to women in leadership positions throughout Cairo, North Africa, and the Middle East.

Chapter 2 contains the outcomes of numerous searches of related literature and discussions relating to the phenomena in the study. The review includes the following sections: (a), women and change (b) women and family, (c) women as leaders, (d) the Arab Spring, (e) status of women, and (f) women and business. The literature review included references from 161 resources. Of the 108 resources, 92 were from peer-reviewed journals and books. The remaining sources were newspaper articles, magazine articles, and non-peer reviewed sources. Some were statistical databases providing information and examples for thorough analysis of the phenomenon.

Title Searches, Articles, Research Documents, and Journals

The researcher conducted searches through the University of Phoenix University Library Internet search engines EBSCOhost, ProQuest, CountryWatch, Emerald, SAGE Knowledge,

SocINDEX, ABI/INFORM Global, ProQuest Digital Dissertations, and ERIC. Internet search engines, Google Scholar, Google, MSN, and Bing were also utilized. Reference and bibliographic listings from related research materials were used to find additional information for literature searches through other university libraries and books online.

The title searches that were used for the purpose of collecting research information included women and leadership, cultural norms and women, leadership theories, women and leadership, women in the Middle East and North Africa, feminist theories, gender role theories, gender roles in the Middle East and North Africa, culture norms and women leaders, stereotypes of Arab women, women and family in the Middle East and North Africa, women and the Arab Spring, Arab Spring and the a number of groupings of these words and phrases.

Women and Change

Women and girls contribute to one-half of all resources in the world. Women in leadership roles vary from country to country and culture to culture. According to *Corporate gender gap report*, the corporate and political worlds are not doing enough to achieve gender equality (Zahidi & Ibarra, 2010). There are significantly less women in leadership positions in the Middle East lower than in other cultures around the world and vary from region to region (Thomas, 2011). A disproportionate number of women compared to men are in leadership and executive management positions in the Middle East, specifically Egypt (DeAnne, Cavanaugh, & Sabbagh, 2011). "The Middle East is a vast, diverse region and the status of women varies significantly from one country to the other ("U.N. speaks up for Mideast women," 2007, para. 5). In some regions women are still faced with discrimination on many fronts and such discrimination is deep-rooted in legal frameworks, educational systems, and culture.

Change in the Middle East is evident more than ever before. Women contributed their leadership skills to the January 25 revolution and continue to be proactive in the cause of democracy, acting as role models and agents of change in their cultural communities (King, 2011). The political upheaval in the Middle East recently has alerted attention to the region. Observers around the world focus on the differences between countries in North America, Europe and the Middle East. The gaps are evident: approximately 35% of women work outside the home, in contrast to about 75% of women in the Western world (Atwater, Wang, Smither, & Fleenor, 2009).

Women and Family

Family laws vary from culture to culture and are subjected to diverse social frameworks in the world today. An examination of family law emphasizes the significance of building perceptions pertaining to Islamic texts on the requirements of present society (Western, 2008). In some places men consider women incapable of doing certain duties, both physically and mentally, and in turn cause some women to question their own competencies. Feminist studies have contributed to the deconstruction of sexuality in the Middle East and they have provided excellent representations of the plight of women in terms of sexual and physical conflict in the Middle East (Agathangelou, 2011).

The article by Agathangelou (2011) offers knowledgeable insights about feminist theories that otherwise are disregarded by researchers in the Middle East. With the assumption that sexuality is at the forefront of conflict between men and women, feminist studies make an attempt to explore the power struggles that exist. However, the question of how women can balance family responsibilities and the rise to the top of their careers and occupations pertains not only to the Middle East (Salih, 2010). The majority of existing models of leadership do not address this phenomenon many women face in their professions around the world.

Unfortunately, women throughout the Middle East are second-class citizens; denied full legal identities by exclusion from the rights, privileges, and security entitled to individuals of society ("U.N. speaks up for Mideast women," 2007). Women do not share the same privileges as men in the Middle East. Discriminatory constitutions, biased mentalities, and unjust laws violate women's rights (Harik & Marsston, 2003). Gender-based violence is still an issue for women in the Middle East. Women are not protected from spousal abuse and the laws (Badran, 2011). Women in Egypt commonly face domestic violence, especially spousal violence. The situation revolves around the subordinate situation women face in both society and family (Harik & Marsston, 2003).

Stigmas are still associated with divorce or previous marriages and women are often discriminated against and at a high risk for abuse (Badran, 2011). These women are physically abused two times the amount as women in their first marriages (Abdel Khalek, 2010). Women of lower classes, the less educated, and poor have a tendency to marry at an early age because of societal and familial pressure (Badran, 2011). Domestic and spousal violence is more common for these women than those who marry later in their lives and have more education. Abdel Khalek (2010), writes " Gender-based violence is more common among less privileged women: women belonging to the lowest wealth quintile are more than twice as likely as those in the highest wealth quintile to experience spousal violence" (Domestic Violence High in Egypt, Affecting Women's Reproductive Health, para. 2). However, no women are immune to domestic or spousal violence (Abdel Khalek, 2010). Honor killings and spousal rape still exist and are not against the law (Abu-Lughod, 2006). While Egypt does not see many cases of this criminal behavior, it is becoming concerning because of the January 25 revolution, and it is on the rise in other countries in the Middle East.

Marriage was considered only a contract to establish an efficient working unit, strengthen alliances, and legitimize children. However, for women the wedding ceremony acted as the transition from child to adult and the commencement of a new role in society (Seawright, 2001). Marriage in ancient Egypt served as the foundation of a tight-knit family unit and a hedge of protection against the inhospitable outside world (Tyldesley, 1994). However all depictions in art, music, and poetry portray the romance of marriage. To marry and produce children was considered a duty of every Egyptian and taken very seriously by all citizens of Egyptian society. This tradition continues in present-day Egypt. Women are expected to marry and bear children and serve their families and husbands (Hoodfar, 1997).

Women as Leaders

The article "Women at the top: Powerful leaders" defines success in terms of work and family in a culture of gender. The authors Cheng and Halpren (2010) review recent research and explore another possible model that indicates and dispels the general belief that men are the prototypical leaders. Cheng and Halpren (2010) challenge the common belief that women are not capable of balancing their family obligations and management of companies. The roles of women in the Middle East convey what men or society deem as acceptable. These positions are generally in the areas of culture, family, women's, issues, marriage, and education (Abu-Lughod, 2006). Exceptions, family ties and succession, pressure from social groups, pressure to appease the West, and commonly or usually appointed positions, play an integral part in the procurement of these positions occupied by women (Youssef, 2002).

The patriarchal nature of the culture and lack of legal literacy both contribute to barriers women face accessing justice systems. The absence of women in leadership roles in politics, private, and public sectors and judiciary positions are a common reality for women (Kamal, March 2011). Women leaders in the Middle East are more discernible than 10 years ago; their influence includes numerous sectors of business, employment, education, and political representation (Kamal, 2011). However, they continue to represent a small minority of these groups and men still dominate in all aspects of society (Atwater, Wang, Smither, & Fleenor, 2009). The integration of women into Egyptian society and their participation in the public sector this century has brought immense changes and the effort to fully include women into all aspects of public life exists (Guenena, n.d.). However, this has been a prolonged process surrounded by controversy.

In an effort to change the perception that other cultures have of the Middle East as oppressive to the female race (Abu-Lughod, 2006), women are attempting to become more active in the attainment of leadership positions. Women aspire to occupy more significant roles through determination, perseverance, and desire to succeed (DeAnne, Cavanaugh, & Sabbagh, 2011). Egyptian women fought courageously with men in the revolution for the resignation of former president Muhammad Hosni Mubarak (Nelson, 2011). These same women are striving for freedom and equality. When women protesters participated in the 18-day Egyptian revolution, men welcomed this new role. It was a significant change from women's traditional responsibility, which was generally limited to the home and family (Durbin, 2011). However, the end of the revolution saw men reverting back and insisting women stay home again.

According to human rights activists, there was a difference between overthrowing a leader and having a social revolution (Durbin, 2011). Women's roles in the uprisings within Egypt were just as important as men's (Nelson, 2011). King (2011) observed that the demonstrations and protests leading to the end of an era with the authoritarian administrate of President Hosni Mubarak saw Egyptian women emerging as leaders and liberators. Women in the Muslim world have hope that they too may become liberated and follow the positions Egyptian women have in their societies (Pessin, 2011).

Almost from the outset of the unrest, Tahrir Square has been a significant and surprising place for women and girls. They are some of the people on the frontlines and are receiving respect at the focal point of the struggle (King, 2011). However they have not used this opportunity to gain leverage in the fight for women's rights. Quite the opposite, they are a part of the massive group of people of both genders who are equal in their fight and purpose (Durbin, 2011). Teenage girls, young children, dignified matrons, and grandmothers made their presence felt and enlarged the crowd at crucial times in the fight against opposition powers (Chick, 2011). Women leaders in the Middle East are more visible than 10 years ago; they influence numerous sectors of business, employment, education, and politics (Kamal, 2011). However, they continue to represent a small minority and men still dominate in most aspects of society (Atwater, Wang, Smither, & Fleenor, 2009).

The Arab Spring

The Arab uprisings, the Arab Spring, started in Tunisia and continued and expanded to other countries in the Middle East and North Africa. The transition in the Arab world has been remarkable and has had an immense effect on the region and will continue to for many generations if not longer (Al Kaylani, 2013). The transformation in the Middle East and North Africa countries is ongoing as people persist in demonstrating for all-encompassing, government, economic and social freedom, substantiated in the notion of equal opportunities for all people (Al

Kaylani, 2013). Both young women and men have been in the forefront of the movement for the transformation to end the complicated cultural norms, social, economic, and legal restrictions. The aforementioned has been a hindrance to women and youth in this part of the world as they strive to find their place and participate completely in and open and fair society (Metcalfe, 2007).

Even prior to the Arab Spring, leaders in the region made some significant changes, giving precedence to job growth within the private sector, broadening and diversifying the economy (Al Kaylani, 2013). In addition, for women and youth, facilitating chances, availabilities, and access to more opportunities for employment, and to start their own businesses. The region has also made substantial investments in education, human resources and development resulting in a closing as much as 90% of the gender gap in education (Al Kaylani, 2013).

Status of Women

Women in Egypt have an extensive and varied history ranging from ancient Egyptian times to the current status they possess today. To understand fully the role of women and their significance in ancient Egyptian society one must start from the Pharaonic era. According to "History of Women in Egyptian Life" (n.d.), Some of the earliest appearances of women in public life in Egypt is the Pharaonic era. Research from this time indicates there was an emphasis of woman's equal status with man where she "enjoyed an equal status with man and engaged in politics and government" (para. 1). Queen Hatshepsut, who reigned from 1479 to 1457 B.C., was one of the more famous queens regarding equality between men and women. She also had a role in enhancing state structure in the areas of religion, trade, and domestic and foreign policy. Nefertiti, Cleopatra, and Shajaret were equally important in later eras ("History of Women in Egyptian Life", n.d.). To understand their moderately open-minded attitudes toward sexual equality, one must realize that the Egyptians regarded their world as a comprehensive duality made of the male and the female. This concept provided orderliness to everything as well as stability (Fletcher, 2011).

Fletcher (2011) writes, "The Egyptians recognized female violence in all its forms, their queens were even portrayed crushing their enemies, executing prisoners or firing arrows at male opponents as well as the non-royal women who stab and overpower invading soldiers" (para. 2). However, Egypt was not an egalitarian society; legal distinctions in Egypt were in terms of differences in the social classes, rather than gender. Rights and privileges were given according to class ("History of Women in Egyptian Life", n.d.).

Harassment is an epidemic that has no prejudices. Egyptian and foreign women alike experience some form of harassment whether it is catcalls and whistling or groping in public places. However, during the demonstrations, women did not experience the sexual harassment that usually occurs. Women could feel safe and secure in a large group of men they usually would shun (Marshall, 2011). In many cases, the law does not support women. Islamic law of *sharia* can be interpreted in various ways. Legal structures and support need to be reformed so that the systems in place include participants of society, especially women (Trofin, & Tomescu, 2010). Education is highly regarded even for women in many countries in the Middle East. Unfortunately, women still represent a small minority in the political process and workforce (Moghadam, 2008). Many of these women are competent, productive, hardworking, and wish to work outside the home. However, the traditional law and patriarchal nature of many countries in the Middle East continue to insist that women must obey any authoritative male family member in the pursuit of work outside the home (Moghadam, 2008).

Women and Business

Economically speaking, young Arabs, both men and women, have been marginalized in most MENA countries (Metcalfe, 2007). Women especially are under-represented in medicine, law, science, finance, engineering, business, media, and sports (*The World Bank: Middle East And North Africa*, 2013). In politics, women hold only 9% of parliament seats throughout the region (Metcalfe, 2008). The World Bank research reports that women only account for 27% of the labor force in the region, and in other low-, middle- and high-income economies women account for 51%. Also in the region only 11% of women are self-employed, compared to 22% of men (Al Kaylani, 2013). At these low levels, it is apparent the rates of participation in region represent massive missed opportunities for development and economic growth in the Arab world (Metcalfe, 2008).

Women striving to make it in the business world throughout MENA countries struggle to gain access to technology, investments, capital , networking, opportunities in marketing, and skills and specialist training (*The World Bank: Middle East And North Africa*, 2013). Thorough out the world cultural attitudes about equality in gender roles, the worth and importance of women's work have an effect on women's participation in the business and economic sectors (Metcalfe, 2008). However, Arab women in the MENA countries are faced with these attitudes, having an especially profound and negative impact on professional choices, entrepreneurship opportunities, and chances of success (Metcalfe, 2008).

The Chauffour (2013) website, reports from the World Bank, and the International Monetary Fund put forward that women in MENA countries who are highly educated are susceptible to unemployment. For example, Al Kaylani (2013) reports "the percentage of young Egyptian women graduating with a university degree rose from 6% to 12% between 1998 and 2006, but the unemployment rate increased from 19% to 27% among young women in the same period of time (para. 9). The Arab International Women's Forum (2010) has indicated the way to development seen as legitimate by others is political empowerment of women in the MENA region. According to Al Kaylani, (2013), "Women's participation in the economy is believed to provide a tremendous impetus to their enhanced participation in public affairs. As yet, the Arab Spring has failed to deliver greater political power to women in the region" (para. 13).

Summary

As Egypt begins a new era and rewrites the constitution, both men and women are attempting to ensure women have more rights. Yet, this is happening in a country steeped in traditional values and after decades this traditionalism is gaining more acceptance and the use of Islamic veils is more frequent than ever before (Badran, 2011). The growing number of women wearing veils is not considered by most Egyptian to be a contradiction against advocating for more women's rights (Pessin, 2011). There is a trend in Cairo for women of all social and economic divisions to adopting the Islamic veil, and there are more women practicing this custom than in the past decades. Almost 100 years ago, women in Egypt fought to discontinue the practice of wearing a veil. Pessin (2011) explained "Well, first of all, the observation is accurate, that there are more women in veils, or behind the veil, than ever there were in modern Egyptian history" (para. 4).

Chapter 3

Methodology

The review of literature disclosed studies on women and leadership in the Middle East and North Africa (MENA). Additionally, the literature offered a historical overview of Egyptian women, and the difficulties they meet regarding the attainment of leadership positions within the patriarchal nature of the culture in Egypt. Very little research addressing women and leadership is this part of the world is available. Few studies were discovered from searches of the ProQuest dissertation database that referred to the lack of women in leadership positions in the Middle East and North Africa, specifically Egypt. Consequently, there is a gap in research that addresses the cultural and social constructs that may hinder Egyptian women's ability to attain to leadership positions in a male dominated society.

The purpose of this qualitative phenomenological study was to fill in the above-mentioned gap by exploring the lived experiences of Egyptian women in positions of leadership as regards to the cultural, social, and patricidal factors that impede their attainment of leadership positions in a male dominated society. The modified van Kaam method proposed by Moustakas (1994),was used in the study to investigate and delve into the experiences, perceptions and viewpoints of 10 Egyptian women in leadership positions. In the study, the exploration of the cultural, social, and patriarchal factors ensued in an effort to determine some of the elements that contribute to the lack of Egyptian females in the positions of leadership in a male dominated society.

In chapter 3, regarding the reasoning for employing a phenomenological qualitative research design and its relevance for the purposes of the research is discussed. Also contained in

Chapter 3 are the research questions, sample population, ethical considerations, the location, the data collection methods, and the instrumentation that was made use of in the study.

Research Design

The modified van Kaam method proposed by Moustakas (1994) was used for the purpose of this qualitative phenomenological study to investigate and examine the views and opinions of a sample of 10 Egyptian women in leadership positions. The intention of the study was to delve into the cultural, social, and patriarchal factors that contribute to the lack of Egyptian females in the positions of leadership in a male dominated society. Qualitative research uses open-ended inquiry to investigate and ascertain a phenomenon, devoid of previous anticipations or expectations of the outcomes (Johnson & Christensen, 2004).

According to Neuman (2003), qualitative studies are dependent on the informative and analytical methodologies of the social sciences and afford an abundance of evidence regarding social processes. The qualitative approach "helps the authors explore a process that has not been examined before and one that displays many complexities" (Creswell, 2008, p. 62).

This study investigates the lived experiences of Egyptian women in roles of leadership in the post Arab Spring atmosphere. The emergence of women leaders in Egypt has begun in force, fuelled by the revolutions, uprisings, and the current condition of the country. The study investigated why some women can break the barrier and procure leadership positions in upper management and supervisory positions in their profession. It also examined why some women are unsuccessful in this endeavor.

Research Method

This research project conducted a qualitative phenomenological study with the intention to explain, explore, and determine the factors that lead to of the emergence of women as leaders in

Egypt. Accomplishing this investigation included the assessment of how participants perceive a condition through experience and consciousness and how it appears in events from a first-person point of view (Groenewald, 2004). The design of research is a crucial process that encompasses the interpretation of a concept of a problematic issue and generating the narrative description (Creswell, 2000). The objective of this qualitative phenomenological study was to identify themes and emerging patterns that may provide opportunities and motivation for women to seek leadership positions and to show how women acquired leadership positions in Egypt today.

Qualitative Method. Qualitative research observes participants in the study in their natural setting where the live, work, or conduct other activities (Creswell, 2008). Qualitative research consists of an investigation that searches for answers to a question, collects evidence, uses a clear set of measures that have been predefined, constructs verdicts not determined beforehand, and are methods outside direct limitations of the study (Neuman, 2006).

Qualitative studies aim to acquire information on cultures, opinions, behaviors, values, and the social structure of specific populations of individuals. Additionally, qualitative research aims to understand a research problem from the perception of the inhabitants it encompasses (Leedy, & Ormond, 2010). The qualitative approach emphasis is on phenomena that transpire in the natural setting of the participant and examining those same phenomena in their complexities and complications that may occur (Creswell, 2008). Qualitative methods will gather information, or introspective interpretations of the researcher, diaries, and protocols (Groenewald, 2004). In this study, the qualitative method investigates the rise of Egyptian women in leadership from the perspective of participants in the study.

Phenomenology. The purpose of the phenomenological approach is to clarify the phenomena based on the perceptions of the participants in the study (Neuman, 2000). The study employed inductive, qualitative methods with the purpose of collecting information from those participating in the study through interviews and discussions (Creswell, 2008). Phenomenology is concerned with the study of experience from the perspective of the individual, "bracketing" taken-for-granted assumptions and usual ways of perceiving (Lester, 1999 p. 1). It is grounded on the notion that the description of the world from one person as felt by the person studied is not either idiosyncratic nor an impartial description.

Phenomenology consequently pursues to explain psychological structures (Starks, 2007). The phenomenological method requires the researcher to look at the data without bias. Therefore it is not suitable to use secondary sources such as literature as a source of data (Starks, 2007). The method's primary mode of collecting data is the interview (Creswell, 2008). This approach is amenable to the present study because it does not require an established theory. The data collection and inductive research method were most appropriate for this study. Inductive reasoning was used as women leaders were interviewed and the results were used to make generalizations about women and leadership.

Appropriateness of Design

The study focused on women in Egypt who were leaders within their organization and the situations they experienced in obtaining these positions. The literature pertaining to this phenomena, especially in Egypt, is sparse and at the same time contradictory on some issues. This is the nature of the Arab culture because of the culture norms pertaining to women. Even though there is some literature on the subject, data previously published indicates a need for more research on women as leaders in Egypt.

The focus of this study was on the lived experiences of Egyptian women in leadership positions therefor; the quantitative research method design was not selected. The quantitative research method is employed to answer questions which the researcher must control, collect numerical data , measure variables, predict, and use statistical procedures to develop a hypotheses and analyze to obtain results from data (Leedy & Ormrod, 2001). The qualitative research method is employed by researchers to answer questions about the nature of phenomena, by describing, understanding, and answering questions from the point of view of the participants' lived experience (Leedy & Ormrod).

By using the qualitative approach, the researcher was able to examine the perspectives of 10 Egyptian women who were in leadership positions. The phenomenological research method purposes is to cultivate a comprehensive, precise, well-defined, and clear explanation and perception of a certain human occurrence or experience (Creswell, 2008). It accomplishes its aim by using an explicit investigator position and methodology and through specific methods of participant selection, inquiry of information, methodical data conduct, and gathering of interview constituents into a final testimony (Groenewald, 2004).

The strength of the phenomenological method is that it provides a description of lived experiences and implications that are rich and complete (Starks, 2007). Results from phenomenological research are given the opportunity to emerge, instead of occurring by the imposition of a researcher (Neuman, 2000). Techniques are employed to retain accounts and descriptions as authentic as possible to the empirical raw data. To accomplish this the researcher must be extremely careful and move specifically one step after the other and take care not to change, distort, delete, or add anything to the original originally presented transcripts from the participant (Groenewald, 2004).

The phenomenological method does have some weaknesses in that its success is contingent on the participant's communicative skills as they provide the facts to the researcher (Creswell, 2008). The inferences and suppositions are dependent on the individual chosen to participate in the study. It is possible to miss information when focusing on a vivid account of an experience, for example what happened before that led to an experience, the consequence or outcome of the experience, or other necessary factors connected to the experience that affected the outcome (Neuman, 2000).

A fundamental aim for doing qualitative research is to acquire an understanding of people's feelings, perceptions, trepidations, and attitudes regarding a specific phenomenon (Yin, 2003). The intent is to obtain direct experience of the phenomenon by interacting with those living the experience. Uncovering details of the phenomenon from the lived perspective of the participants is a primary purpose of phenomenological research (Creswell, 2005; Neuman, 2003).

The aim of the research was to investigate and explore the perceptions, beliefs, and attitudes of the lived experiences of a sample of 10 Egyptian women who are in leadership positions. According to Neuman (2003), in-depth investigation purposive sampling is effective so the researcher can inquire about specific participants' knowledge with the purpose of gaining a greater understanding of the subject scientific evidence is "derived from first- person reports of life experiences" (Moustakas, 1994, p. 84). Moustakas' modified van Kaam method was employed to analyze data and was appropriate for this study because the perceptions and lived experiences of Egyptian women in leadership positions and how they acquired these positions were explored. A qualitative rather than quantitative study was more applicable for this research due to the nature of the study. According to Creswell (2003) specific elements help determine if a qualitative or quantitative research design would be most appropriate for a study.

Qualitative research methods are based more on the interpretation and providing views, looking at contexts, and an in-depth of understanding of concepts (Berg, 2007). Quantitative research is usually considered to be the more "scientific" approach to doing social science (Berg, 2007 p. 77). The concentration of quantitative research is on employing definitions that are specific and vigilantly operationalizing what certain variables and concepts mean (Tewksbury, 2009).

In quantitative studies, problems come forward in the literature, variables are identified, and theories are tested and confirmed to build connections and relationships. In contrast, qualitative studies explore a research problem in an effort to understand and develop concepts and theories to shape a hypothesis to test (Tewksbury, 2009). The variables in qualitative research generally are not known, and the researcher focuses on the perspective that may offer understanding of a phenomenon (Creswell, 2008).

Population

The sample population represents people who share characteristics categorized under common groups (Creswell, 2008). The population sample for this study consisted of women leaders, scholars, and executives in Egypt. The foundational belief systems of groups or individuals made up of principles and tenets that are not easily altered. The mindset of a person is a conjectural construct that characterizes the individual's partialities or aversions. The effect of a person's values may influence viewpoints and conduct is not explicitly linked to the intellectual process (Black, 1999). It is important to choose the right subjects for the interview process, "the standard in choosing participants and sites is whether they are "information rich"" (Creswell, 2008, p. 204). Phenomenological studies require that one makes sure participants have experiences that reflect the required data for the research questions, and to assure information collected is reliable (Faÿ & Riot, 2007).

Sampling

Techniques were used to maintain continuity in characteristics of the people in the study similar to the population at large. With this particular population in Egypt, samples must have been available and willing to participate (Salkind, 2003). Sampling in qualitative research is often misunderstood to imply that sample size is of no importance (Onwuegbuzie & Leech, 2005). The primary reason for this belief is qualitative researchers are often apathetic in generalizing to underlying populations (Onwuegbuzie & Leech). Cottrell (2005), indicated an adequate sample size in qualitative research is a judgment decision for the researcher to make. Creswell (2008), maintained that sample size in qualitative research must be sufficient enough to enable analysis that is thorough and methodical, a feature of all qualitative inquiry. Ten Egyptian women in leadership positions were used in the study with the purpose of generating different responses, obtaining plentiful and rich meanings, and collect quality data (Onwuegbuzie & Leech, 2005).

One criteria-based method for choosing a sample is snowball sampling. In this method, the participants in the study are asked to identify people that might be appropriate to become a part of the sample (Creswell, 2008). A benefit of the technique is that it enables the researcher to engage numerous appropriate participants for the study (Creswell, 2005). It does however have disadvantages as it might put parameters on the participants and result in small network of candidates (Polit & Beck, 2006).

I asked women in positions of leadership that I have previously known and used a non-probability sampling technique, and snowball sampling, to expand the sample. Snowball sampling was an appropriate technique to employ to find potential subjects. In this particular situation, considering the cultural constraints, subjects were hard to locate. From the sample frame, participants were randomly chosen to ensure equality in the selection process (Creswell, 2008).

Qualitative research's intention is to understand a specific phenomenon. However there are designs that are specific for qualitative designs for certain conditions and aims. Two of the designs are the ethnographic and the grounded theory approach. The ethnographic approach dictates that the researcher immerses him or herself completely into a social group that is being studied for the purpose of gaining a good understanding the phenomena. The grounded theory approach directs the researcher to develop a theory based on the findings of a question as to why a certain phenomenon transpires (McDuffie & Scruggs, 2008). The ethnographic design was not appropriate for this study as the phenomenon under investigation was not restricted to a social group; the women experienced the phenomenon differently from one another. The grounded theory was not appropriate as the focus was discover the nature of the phenomena as it occurs without seeking out a theory to explain it.

Another qualitative design is the case study approach. This approach aims to explore a connection and find the fundamental principles through an illustrative, investigative, or descriptive analysis of a group, event, or person (Yin, 2009). The case study was not appropriate for this study because the researcher could not give response to information given by the participants instead of exploring the phenomenon as it transpires.

The approach that was most appropriate for this study was the phenomenological approach as it afforded the researcher opportunity for collecting a comprehensive understanding of the lived experiences and perceptions of women leaders in Egypt. In this approach, it was essential that the researcher was open to themes that emerged from the research without bias, judgment, or presuppositions (Finlay, 2008). Specific groups have experiences that are true to their nature, the phenomenological approach allows the researcher the ability to gain insight to these experiences (Walker, Cooke, & McAllister, 2008).

For the purpose of this study, an interview was used to collect data from the participants. Open-ended questions, according to Creswell (2008), allow the participants to elaborate on their responses and offers unlimited possibilities for the participants to provide for each question. "Phenomenological, human scientific researchers tend to choose the interview due to their interest in the meaning of a phenomenon as it is lived by other subjects" (Englander, 2012, p. 14). The interviews were conducted over the phone using a set of questions that were predetermined and allowed the participant to elaborate expanding the dialogue.

Informed Consent

The participants in the study were asked to sign an informed consent form prearranged by the researcher. Shank (2006), emphasizes the use of informed consent helps uphold the ethical standards the researcher must observe: to proceed with utmost caution, doing no harm, and being approachable and trustworthy. The name and purpose of the study are included in an informed consent letter. Also included in the letter is a description of the process for the interview and follow-up procedures. The letter included the assurance of confidentiality, and a notification that they may withdrawal at any point of the study. For the purpose of maintaining the confidentiality agreement, interview transcriptions, and informed consent forms were separated. The participants were given a number to replace their names in the interest of retaining the assurance of anonymity.

Prior to submitting my application to IRB, all protocols in place were followed, including receiving an initial approval from committee members, who directed me to submit for IRB (a process required by the University of Phoenix). The informed consent form was a required document as part of the application. Following the acceptance from the IRB, I was able to continue with the process of submitting my dissertation.

Instrumentation

Designing an instrument, revising an instrument that previously has been used, or selecting a prefabricated instrument are different ways to develop an instrument. Various methods of interview protocols can be designed to produce an abundant amount of facts necessary for a qualitative investigational perspective (Creswell, 2008). To ensure consistent and common information is collected from the interviewee, the guide approach was used to provide a focus for the researcher and participants. This approach permitted a certain amount of autonomy and flexibility to acquire the appropriate information from the interviewee.

The interviews consisted of presenting open-ended questions to allow women to reflect on their success in obtaining leadership positions and remaining in these positions. Phenomenological theorist Edmund Husserl was the world renowned founder of phenomenology in the twentieth century. Phenomenological studies seek intentional, conscious, quality, and first-person perspectives on the issue at hand (Lester, 1999). There are particular fundamental features in an individual's life sociality, sense of selfhood, spatiality, personification, temporality, development, dialogue, and preference or disposition of surroundings that best suit the participants; therefore interviews were conducted in natural settings. These interwoven elements acted as a perspective on the data collected (Ashworth, 2003).

In this study, the interviewer is a vital, most important component of the research process and is the primary instrument of the study (Patton 2002). This notion of the 'researcher as research instrument' is significantly contingent on the worldview of the researcher and the epistemological, ontological, and axiological foundations of what represents acceptable research (Merriam, 2002).

In-depth interviews offer a more relaxed environment affording participants a comfortable atmosphere to answer questions and have a conversation about them. There are, however, issues associated with in-depth interviews that should be considered. In-depth interviews are disposed to bias. There is a danger of the person interviewing the participants to ask or skew the question in a way that elicits a favorable response pertaining to the study. Participant can also have a bias because they want to give the "right" answer that relates to the topic and appear impressive to the researcher. As a researcher it is important to control one's reactions. The interviewer's goal is to determine a person's views and interpretations of the world around them. Collecting data and investigating settings were conducted in the interviewee's natural environment in the hopes of acquiring authentic, substantive, and in depth data (Merriam, 2002).

The following questions will guide the interviews:

1. How long have you been in your current position and how long were you in previous positions that facilitated your achievement of obtaining this position?

2. What factors if any did familial affiliations or other individuals known to you have in the process of procurement of your position?

3. What role did your education or previous training play in regard to your qualifications for the position?

4. How many women, if any, currently hold positions of equal or more power in your organization?

5. Is there any female person or persons you mentor or help by providing guidance and advice and what are her future goals?

Interview Protocol

A standardized, open-ended interview will be employed and all interviews will be audio recorded. The interview is focused but permits the interviewer some autonomy to obtain information. The standardized, open-ended interview asked the same questions to the participants yet still allows them to answer in their own words (Gall, Gall, & Borg, 2003). In-depth interviewing is a rigorous process that allows an individual to investigate his or her viewpoints on a specific idea, system, or condition. The technique involves a small amount of participants with the goal of gaining a clearer grasp of the phenomenon in the research (Boyce & Neale, 2006). To obtain specified information about women in Cairo and leadership positions, new issues, opinions, and actions were explored in depth. Patton (2002) deems it the responsibility of the interviewer "to be sensitive to how the interviewee may be affected by different questions and various question formats" (p. 129).

The interviewer should begin an interview by asking a number of factual or forthright questions to foster a sense of security for the participant. Questions of this type are proposed to elicit straightforward descriptions, actions, behaviors, or experiences with the purpose of fostering participants to use descriptive forms of speech (Faÿ & Riot, 2007). Patton (2002) argues that opinions and feelings, which are linked to this descriptive information, are more likely to be accurate, as the respondent has "just verbally relived the experience" (p. 120).

Data Collection Procedures

The data collection process involved interviews that encapsulated the perspectives of the participants of the study. The sample size of the study consisted of 10 women and each participant was interviewed two times each for 30 minutes. Follow-up questions took place face to face or via phone or e-mail. Following the norms of the culture, no men were interviewed for this study. It would be inappropriate for a woman researcher to ask a man questions about women in leadership positions.

In-depth interviewing is a process involving a rigorous interview process to investigate viewpoints on a specific idea, system, or condition. The technique involves a small amount of participants with the objective of procurement a better grasp of the phenomenon in the study (Boyce &Neale, 2006). Women leaders and those striving to become leaders were the sample group for interviews. Their opinions on specific issues pertinent to women in Cairo and leadership positions were explored in depth.

Data Analysis Procedures

According to Merriam (2009), "Qualitative researchers are interested in understanding the meaning people have constructed, that is, how people make sense of their world and the experiences they have in the world" (p. 13). The objective of phenomenological research is to remain unbiased, the researcher carefully and thoroughly examines the data. Careful examination of data guided an assimilation of all feedback connected to the interview questions.

Descriptions, interpretations of the data, and analysis are extremely important for reporting the conclusions of this qualitative research. The innovation and implications of data collected are a crucial component of the researches conclusions (Creswell, 2008). It is essential the researcher identifies why and how the investigation and interpretations were composed. For this study, an audio device was used to record responses to five interview questions. The responses were transcribed, analyzed, coded, separated, and placed in a file specifically for each participant in the study.

Moustaka's (1994) systematic approach to chunking and managing data is a precise method for phenomenological data analysis. This is a rigorous approach that is devised to eradicate researcher bias (Creswell, 2008). Every statement that is relevant to the questions asked in the study was analyzed, creating meaning units, which were then clustered and organized for creating categories. Themes can then be created regarding relations across categories.

The bracketing of personal beliefs and experiences of Egyptian women in leadership positions was essential to circumvent any preconceptions. The epoché stage is where beliefs and assumptions are documented and then consciously set aside, so it was essential to bracket all preconceived notions about the phenomenon as possible. This permitted the essences of the Egyptian women in leadership positions who participated in the study experiences to emerge. Epoching allows the mind to open and become an effective receptacle of the experience of participants. Themes were then synthesized and the experiences of the participants were described in textual and structural forms. The researcher then created a compound explanation of the experience through meanings and the essences (Moustakas, 1994).

Judgments, opinions, and perceptions were put aside to allow the researcher to generate a new perspective on the data. Identifying existing perceptions and beliefs, and cataloging judgments with the intention to place these ideas aside for the extent of the research process was important to avoid researcher bias (Moerer-Urdahl & Creswell, 2004). Examining and identifying significant statements about the participants' experiences from the research data was essential (Moerer-Urdahl & Creswell, 2004). Statements that were identified were placed in a table to enable the researcher to view the statements together and arrange an unencumbered synopsis of the range of responses (Moustakas, 1994). The statements were reported as verbatim statements from the participants, and are not categorized in any way (Moerer-Urdahl & Creswell, 2004). This phase of the process created a horizon to present depth and character to the phenomenon (Moustakas, 1994).

Eliminating statements that were irrelevant or redundant to the phenomenon under study provided a clear view (Moerer-Urdahl & Creswell, 2000). The statements, or horizons, that remained were grouped by major themes and the individual statements evaluated and placed with correlated statements to form the theme and afford a greater understanding of participants' lived experiences (Moustakas, 1994). Both what was experienced and how it was experienced by the participants afford structural and textural descriptions applicable to the themes and horizons, providing a framework and perspectives on the themes that resulted from the interviews.

Validity and Reliability

Validity is defined in qualitative studies by an array of terminologies. There is no specific, set, or general perception of the concept. Instead, validity is "rather a contingent construct, inescapably grounded in the processes and intentions of particular research methodologies and projects" (Winter, 2000, p. 1). Many researchers agree there needs to be a qualifying assessment or gauge for qualitative research. Creswell & Miller (2000) propose that the perception of researchers affects the validity through the selection of paradigms and suppositions, resulting in researchers developing their own theory of validity. Researchers have created or adopted terms they deem as appropriate, for example, quality, rigor, and trustworthiness (Golafshani, 2003).

Shank (2006) connects validity with truth examined. Groenewald (2004) explained that to ensure and check validity, participants are allowed to review the information they provided for accuracy. Interview questions that are inadequately constructed in a study result in insufficient validity (Creswell, 2008).

In-depth interviews are advantageous because they allow the interviewer to ask open-ended and semi-structured questions that provide more comprehensive data than other types of collection methods. They also afford a more comfortable environment for the participants and provide an atmosphere for collecting information. There are, however; limitations and drawbacks to this particular technique of acquiring data; it is disposed to bias and can take more time than other methods.

The participants were provided with the transcript of their individual interview to ensure the depictions of their lived experiences were expressed truthfully and authentically. Validity is associated with the observation of truth (Shank, 2006). Allowing participants to check the information they provided to the researcher helps ensure the validity of the data (Groenewald, 2004). Questions that are not constructed adequately will result in a study with poor validity (Creswell, 2008). Thorough consideration in creating questions will also increase the study's validity (Polit & Beck, 2006).

Currently the political situation in Cairo is unstable resulting in an atmosphere that at times can be aggressive. As a foreigner, particularly an American woman, living in Cairo can be challenging. It was important for the researcher to respect and follow cultural expectations, observing the male/female dynamic. The interview questions in the study were designed with respect and sensitivity to the current situation in Cairo. Egyptians are private people and generally do not converse about their lives with people other than family and friends. Therefore, it was a challenge to find women for the sample group to interview. It was important to reassure the participants that information will be used for the study only. Every effort was be made to make the participants comfortable.

Reliability is generally a concept employed for examining or assessing quantitative research; however, the design is also used in qualitative research. When one looks at the concept of assessing as a way of extracting information, it is a crucial element for a qualitative study to test for quality. A worthy qualitative study can aid one to "understand a situation that would otherwise be enigmatic or confusing" (Golafshani, 2003, p. 601). According to, Stenbacka, (2001) "the concept of reliability is even misleading in qualitative research. If a qualitative study is discussed with reliability as a criterion, the consequence is rather that the study is no good" (p. 552).

Conversely, Patton (2001) maintains both validity and reliability are features a researcher should pay attention to and employ as he or she is designing, judging, and analyzing the results and quality a qualitative study. This correlates to the query "How can an inquirer persuade his or her audiences that the research findings of an inquiry are worth paying attention to?" (Golafshani, 2003, p. 601). To make certain there is reliability in qualitative research, trustworthiness is a crucial aspect and must be examined (Golafshani, 2003). Seale (2002) established that in qualitative research reliability and validity are essential for quality studies and states that the "trustworthiness of a research report lies at the heart of issues conventionally discussed as validity and reliability" (p. 266). To expand the scope of perception of reliability and show the congruency of reliability and validity in qualitative research, Seale (2002) asserts that: "Since there can be no validity without reliability, a demonstration of the former [validity] is sufficient to establish the latter [reliability;]" (p. 316).

Ethical Considerations

Moral value basis refers to the motivation to perform in a morally correct manner. Individuals face ethical dilemmas every day and they influence one's conduct and character. The researcher has an obligation both morally and professionally to conduct his or her research in an ethical manner in the midst of dilemmas, conflict, and concerns that may arise in the process. (Neiburg-Terkle, 1992).

Ethical considerations are a set of rules, standards, or regulation to guide a profession or individual in right behavior. Any institution that has confidentiality agreements has ethical responsibilities, but not all ethical considerations are governed by law. Research is important; however, anonymity of people participating is essential unless otherwise specified. Consent occurs when a person gives permission to release records, participants in research, or offers personal information.

Summary

From the beginning of this study careful and diligent care and consideration was taken to protect the identity of the participants. All discussions, interview transcripts, and field notes on each person were kept separate and only the researcher and participant had access to the documents pertaining to the study. Interviews were conducted in a private, non-disclosed place, and only the researcher and the individual being interviewed had knowledge of the meeting taking place. All steps were taken to protect the identity of the participants and nature of the research topic.

Chapter 4

Results

The purpose of this study was to investigate the perceptions and lived experiences of women emerging as leaders in Egypt. As a qualitative phenomenological study, it focused on the "subjectivity of reality, continually pointing out the need to understand how humans view themselves and the world around them" (Willis, 2007, p. 53). Moustakas explains, "Evidence from phenomenological research is derived from that person's reports of life experiences" (p. 84).

Women's rights and their relationship to leadership roles becomes complicated in a country in political turmoil. Women were involved many positions during the Arab Spring, however; the influence this has had on women's rights is still ambiguous (El-Dabh, 2013). The participation and commitment of women in the Arab Spring evolved further than just partaking in street protests. Women helped to organize and lead protestors, and they played an active part in providing crucial information to the social media outlets, radically participating in cyberactivism (Charles & Denman 2012). They used social media outlets such as Facebook, YouTube, Twitter, e-mail, texting, and podcasts in a vital way to communicate expeditiously to a significant number of people (Newsom & Lengel, 2012).

Women of all social classes and generations joined the masses in Tahrir Square. At checkpoints, just as the men frisked other men, women did the same to other women. Prior to this movement, women were not inclined to participate in protests because both police and male protestors harassed women verbally and sexually. Asmaa Mahfouz posted a video on Facebook and YouTube on January 18, 2012 announcing, "Whoever says women shouldn't go to protests because they will get beaten, let him have some honor and manhood and come with me on January 25" (Morgan, 2011, p. 1). A group on Facebook group called Women of Egypt compiled photos depicting the roles of women in the protests. They showed women brandishing clubs and bats, patrolling the streets in their neighborhoods and providing protection following the disappearance of security forces (Morgan, 2011).

Women's participation in the Arab Spring circumvented general cultural attitudes toward them as they were involved in all aspects of the revolution. Not only did they participate but also were leaders and organizers of protests. After the Arab Spring, many expected continuation ofefforts prtaining to women rights in a county that continues to discriminate against them. However; the hopes of women activists did not materialize; the revolution did not have the desired impact on the role of women (El-Dabh, 2013).

Results from the data compiled from the interviews indicate that women continue to strive for positions of leadership, yet the patriarchal nature of the culture continues to dominate political factions. Women's rights are not considered to be a priority for Islamist or liberal parties. None of the political parties supported the implementation of a quota for women in parliament (World Wide Human Rights Movement, n.d.). Islamists have taken control of the state and there have been many changes in the government. This development has raised concerns among a large number of residents of Cairo that these new parties and changes in government threaten the women's movement. The Muslim Brotherhood stated "increasing recognition of women's rights could be detrimental to society, indicating a return to a more patriarchal structure of society where women would not be allowed to travel, work, use contraception without her husband's approval, or manage the family's finances" (FIDH-World Wide Human Rights Movement, para. 7).

Framework for Presentation of Data

Information was assembled through open-ended interviews of 10 women in leadership positions ranging from high to low. As indicated by Creswell, it is pertinent to "ask open-ended and broad questions that will enable the participants to share their views about the problem being studied" (Creswell, 2008, p. 145). The phenomenological scheme incorporates distinguishing aspects of the participants' experiences as well as their perceptions as they view the phenomenon (Giorgi, 2006). Perspectives from the participant's point of view were collected to the point that the level of saturation had been reached, and there was no more relevant data available (Moustakas, 1994). With the phenomenological aim of returning to the concrete, captured by the slogan 'Back to the things themselves!' (Groenewald, 2004 p. 5), interviews were transcribed and acted as a guide to formulate emergent themes that materialized in the analysis of the data (Creswell, 2008).

Chapter 1 offered the necessary introduction to the study, a conceptual framework, an overview of gender and leadership theories, a historical survey, and definitions of terms. Chapter 2 presented the theoretical perspective, a review of the literature, and a summary of the status of women in Egyptian society. Chapter 3 explained the design and methodology of the study, described the procedures for the selection of participants, instrumentation, data collection, data analysis procedures, limitations and delimitations of the study, and ethical considerations.

Chapter 4, the present chapter, includes the presentation and application of the fundamental procedures of phenomenological studies as explained by horizontalization, clusters of meaning, textural description, and structural design. These essential protocols are derived from the methodical framework of Moustakas (1994), who adapted the modified seven-point method of analysis developed by van Kaam. The seven points included in van Kaam's method are horizontalization, reduction, validation, individual description, textural description, structural description, and textural-structure description. Moustakas' (1994) method begins with the task of ascertaining the phenomenon to study, followed by bracketing experiences by way of interviews to collect data from individuals who have experienced the phenomenon being studied. The data is analyzed by gathering the information, reducing it into important summary statements, and bringing them together to formulate themes. The researcher develops a textural description from the experiences as experienced by the participants and creates a structural description of how they experienced and perceived their environment, situations and circumstances. Textural and structural descriptions are combined to express the experience's essence (Moustakas, 1994). Moustakas maintained that his modified version of the analysis procedure delivers and unveils the data in a way that pinpoints the important, significant themes within the findings.

The study will reveal data that describes how Egyptian women perceive through lived experience the factors that led to of their emergence as leaders in Egypt. The data framework is presented in Figure 1 and reflects Moustakas' modification of van Kaam's seven-point method of analyzing the data (1994).

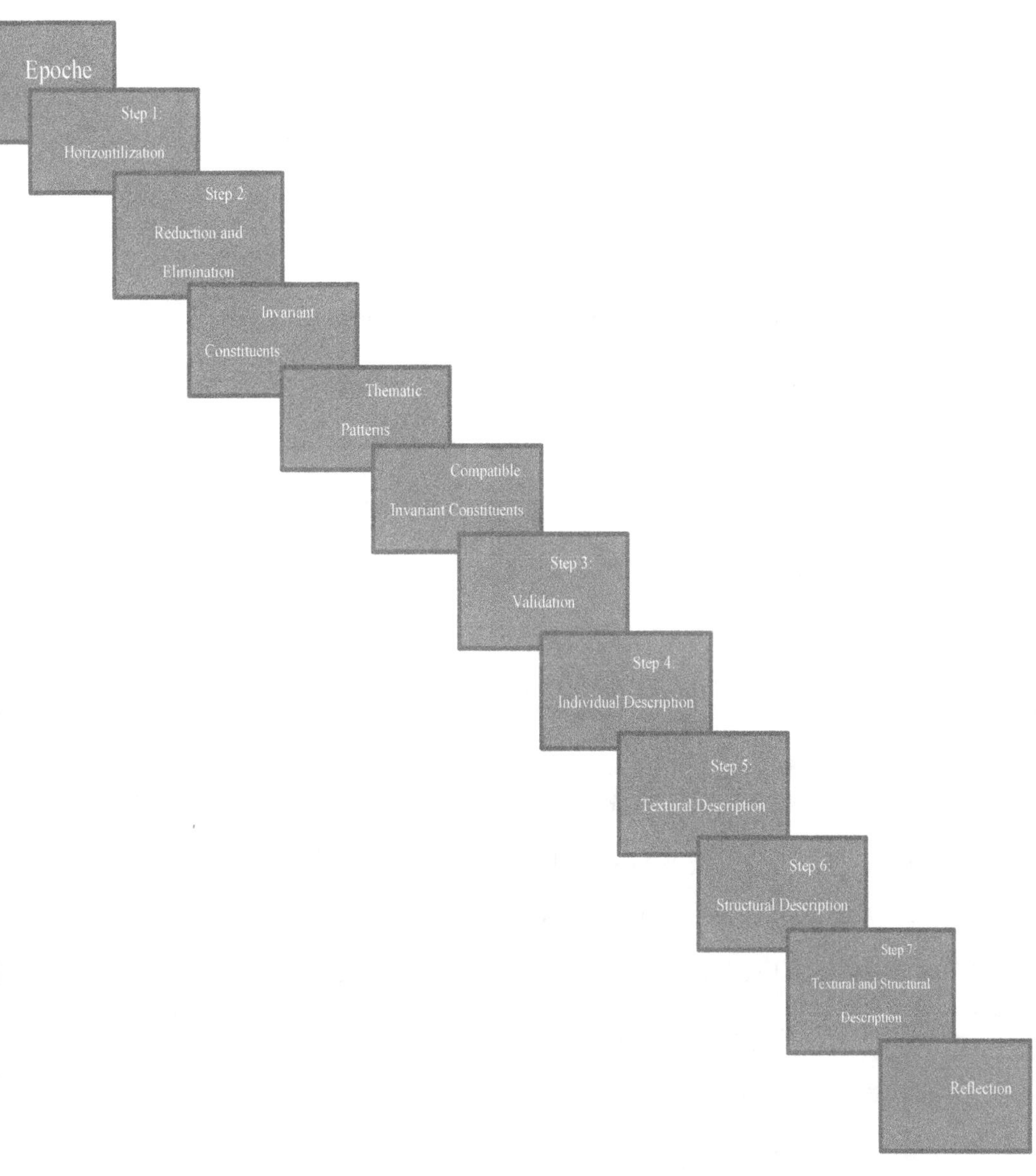

Figure 1. Flowchart of the framework of data presentation.

Data Collection

The collection of data entailed asking each participant open-ended questions with the purpose of acquiring an understanding of their lived experiences of women leaders in Egypt. In-depth interviewing was used with the intention of "gathering data that will lead to a textural description and a structural description of the experiences, and ultimately provide an understanding of the common experiences of the participants" (Creswell, p. 61). Creswell (1998) advised the researcher to obtain subjects that are available without difficulty as in- depth interviews are comprehensive and extensive, making it necessary to interview participants more than once.

Interview Protocol

Ten Egyptian women between the ages of 30-50 participated in the study and the open-ended interview questions and answers were recorded. Interviews consisted of five questions and took anywhere from 30-40 minutes each. "The length of a phenomenological interview is guided by the process of saturation, i.e. when the narratives become repetitive and no new data is revealed. When data saturation is reached, then sampling will stop" (Mapp, 2008 p. 310).

After receiving the signed informed consent forms, the interviews were scheduled. The interviews were administered and recorded with an audio device. The open-ended questionnaire method allowed the women in the study to give individual viewpoints, offer their understanding of their experiences, and share their sentiments in their continuing roles of leadership in the post Arab Spring atmosphere.

Two groups of the participants were established for the organization of the clusters: women aged 25-38 and women over 40. The examination of the data was continuous until saturation was reached: there were no new issues or themes as regard to the grouping of data. When all of the groups were formed and checked for validity, the review was discontinued.

The individual transcriptions of the data were made and each participant received transcriptions of the recorded data from their interview. The transcriptions were sent via e-mail to the participants for review, authentication, and interpretation to verify content. The participants were requested to make additions or corrections as they deemed necessary to ensure authenticity. A second interview was scheduled and conducted for each participant and, after careful review of the transcribed material, any necessary changes were discussed and noted.

Research Questions

What are the implications from lived experiences Egyptian women face in their continuing roles of leadership in the post Arab Spring atmosphere?

1. What are the perceived factors that contribute to the lack of women acquiring positions of management, guidance, and leadership?

2. What are the perceived positions of leadership women occupy the most?

More men than women are the leaders, politicians, and activists in Egypt and fewer women have the opportunity to obtain these roles. The issues that influence the shortage of women acquiring positions of management, guidance, and leaders will be explored. For women to obtain leadership position the question regarding how the positions were acquired will be studied.

Interview Questions

The questions asked in the interview were designed so the researcher could understand, analyze, and relate the lived experiences of the respondents in their roles as women in leadership in Egypt. The questions disclosed the participants' attitudes, feelings, and experiences as they perceive them. The interviews were informal and conducted over the phone. The interview questions are presented in Appendix A.

Data Presentation

The interviews consisted of five questions aimed at drawing out information pertaining to the perceptions these women have concerning family, leadership, and the symbiotic role they play in their everyday lives. For the collection of pertinent data and sound analysis to take place, two purposeful questions are essential: (a) "What have you experienced in terms of the Phenomenon? And, (b) "What contexts or situations have typically influenced or affected your experience? (Creswell, 2008, p. 61). Creswell elaborates: "Other open-ended questions may be asked, but these two, especially, focus attention on gathering data that will lead to a textual…and structural description of the experiences, ultimately provide an understanding of the common experiences of the participants" (Creswell, 2008, p. 61). Asking the participant what they experienced in relation to the phenomenon and asking what situations or settings have influenced or affected their experience assists with the collection of important data for analysis.

The first step in the data presentation necessitated examining the data gathered from both interviews for the purposes of extracting information pertinent to the participants' perceptions, opinions, and attitudes regarding their experiences as women leaders in Egypt.

Analysis of Data

The data in this study is presented by engaging van Kaam's seven-point approach from Moustakas' (1994) adapted methodology with the purpose of identifying the themes and patterns conveyed in the researcher's interviews. This approach provided essential components of the research design of this investigation. The following is a lexicon of the core terms pertaining to Moustakas' methodology.

Bracketing. Husserl's method of epoché or "bracketing" was developed around 1906 and considered to be a radicalization of the methodological constraint (Hurssel, 1973). Hurssel's self-professed Cartesianism is seen by some as an exaggeration. Husserl actually broke free from the Cartesian project in modern philosophy. Husserl's gradual development toward transcendental idealism between 1900 and 1913 may be seen as a progressive radicalization of the Cartesian requirement of finding an indubitable foundation of knowledge by means of the method of doubting (Giorgi, 2009). Summarizing the argument of his lectures in 1907, Husserl wrote that he wanted to "grasp purely and develop consistently what was already implied in this very old intention" of Cartesian doubt that took place in five or six steps (Hurssel, 1928).

In his *Logical Investigations* Hurssel provided, an accurate phenomenological description implemented from a the point of view of the first person, with the purpose of making certain that the experienced item is described by the subject. The concept of horizontalization involves the consideration that each statement in the beginning is to be valued equally (Mustakas, 1994) Statements unrelated to the question or topic, repetitive, or overlapping are removed. Non-repetitive and non-overlapping constituents are grouped into themes thus creating invariant qualities and themes. Finding thematic patterns involves collecting data from interviews, identifying that information as it relates to patterns already established, and combining correlated patterns into sub-themes (Aronson, 1994).

Horizontalization. The examination of the data procedure consisted of two components. The first component concentrated on the horizontalization of repetitious and ambiguous replies that were inconsequential to the horizontal experience. The second component involved the elimination of recurring experiences to remove unnecessary data. This assists in the ability to analytically evaluate, manage, and decipher the data. According to Moustakas (1994), this process is essential to expose the accurate or fundamental concepts for a distinct comprehension of the experiences provided by participants.

Creswell (1998) indicated that phenomenological data analysis follows the same steps and are comparable. Even though they have different methodologies, they employ similar fundamental steps. Horizontalization is the first original protocol of this approach (Creswell, 1994). Horizontalization necessitates distancing the situation, making elements equal, and looking at it without expectations, assumptions, or biases. Next, the clusters of meaning are taken and developed into themes or groups using the significant statements of the participants. This grouping ensures that textural description is achieved after which results are composed. A conventional account of the participants' experiences is constructed. The textural description is the experience expressed through the structural description (Moerer-Urdahl & Creswell, 2004). The steps of this study built upon one another and gave it the qualities of an inductive study (Rudestam & Newton).

Reduction and elimination. Moustakas' (1994) described the third step in his data analysis model stating "phenomenological reflection and imaginative variation" (p. 257). Moustakas (1994) recommends that, to accomplish a reflective and imaginative likeness, the researcher is to use the individual textural descriptions to explain experiences according to analysis of descriptions given by participants in the study. In addition, measurement of the lived experiences is achieved more by synthesizing data through reducing and eliminating information pertaining to the themes that emerged from the transcriptions of the interviews. Moustakas (1994), by way of review, says a participant's expression must meet two prerequisites: "(a) does it contain a moment of the experience necessary and sufficient constituent for understanding it and (b) is it possible to abstract and label it?" (p. 120).

The descriptions of the experience were subject to elimination if they did not meet these requirements. The invariant constituents emerged as the central themes of the experience during the coding, clustering, and thematizing process. Moustakas (1994) states "The clustered and labeled constituents are the core themes of the experience" (p. 121). The reduction and elimination phase reduced and eliminated experiences of no use to the study.

Validity. Validation is, according to Moustakas (1994), an evaluation of the themes associated with the invariant constituents and compared to the complete transcription of the women in the study. It necessitates taking the data from the first step and analyzing and assessing the information to ascertain if it holds pertinent information of experiences of the women vital to the perception of their experiences. Moustakas describes the outcome as a kind of measurement of scope or horizon. Groenewald, (2004) states, "At this point a 'validity check' is conducted by returning to the informant to determine if the essence of the interview has been correctly 'captured' any modification necessary is done as result of this 'validity check'" (p. 20).

Individual descriptions. Identifying the primary themes is part of the presentation of data in steps 4 and 5. Thematic portrayal is effective in the phenomenological methodology put forth by Moustakas (1994). The result of precisely transcribing the interviews and extracting information that directly represents the participant's lived experiences is pertinent in the analysis of the data.

The fourth step of Moustakas' (1994) method uses the individual textural description to analyze the data. It entails forming a textural description of each of the lived experiences of the women, taken exactly as it is expressed from the recorded interviews. The integrated individual and group structural description is the sixth step and is taken from the analysis of the data. This step is described by Creswell (1998) "an exhaustive description of the essential invariant structure (or essence) of the experience" (p. 176).

The data presentation in the sixth step used the textural description, taking the exact words as said by the participants, to convey instances of the experiences they lived. For example, one participant stated, "Women have begun to make progress in roles of leadership experiences; however, much of the traditional cultural values prevail." The data presentation of the sixth step was focused the participants past and current experience. The individual structural description in the sixth step was essential in showing a precise account of the participants' descriptive explanation of the experiences.

Textural-structural description. For the data presentation in the final step, the seventh step, Moustakas (1994), recommended a group composite description. The seventh step is the apex of the examination of phenomenological analysis it integrates the information collected and shows the importance and quintessence of the experiences of the women in the study.

The statements and themes classified as significant were used to write an account of the participants' experiences creating the textural description. In addition, the statements were used to devise an explanation of the framework or setting that shaped the way the phenomenon was experienced by the participants. This is called the structural description. A modified version of Moustakas method is more structured, using supplementary levels in the data reduction process, making it more effective than van Kaam's seven- step method. Not only does it contend that the only thing that one definitely knows is derived from our consciousness but also that this information ensures its objectivity (Moerer-Urdahl & Creswell, 2004).

The emergence of phenomena as seen to one in his or her consciousness comprises the scientific study of phenomenology (Moustakas', 1994). The 'phenomenon' is an appropriate preliminary point for reflection and consideration. The explanation of the phenomenon in terms of probable consequences and constituents is formed when the appearance of an object in one's consciousness come together with the object as it appears its natural setting. According to Moustakas (1994), "what appears in consciousness is an absolute reality while what appears to the world is a product of learning" (p. 27). Subsequently, one can distinguish the attributes of consciousness and comprehend of the fundamental nature of the experience. Essentially, the object does not need to be existent at the time; it makes no difference; objects can appear in one's consciousness.

Demographic Data

The demographics for every participant was documented before the initiation of the interview. Participants were given a code number to protect their identity and ensure anonymity. The women interviewed were between 33 and 54 years old with an average age of approximately 42 years. Five of these women were over 40 (50%) and five were between the ages of 30-37 (50%). All of the women had graduated from university and most had degrees in higher education. Three of the women worked in educational institutions, one of these is the medical director in an educational institution (30%), two in corporate positions (20%), one in the medical field (10%), and four worked in the family business (40%). Most of the women who worked for non-family businesses had a supervisor to which they reported. Two of these women were not necessarily supervised but were still responsible to the owner of the company (20%). Of the three women who worked for their families, they all had main supervisory positions (30%). Again, these women ultimately had to answer to a board of directors or owner. Five of the women obtained their particular positions without the aid of any outside sources, family or otherwise (50%). They went through the application and interview processes. One participant said that although no one in her family procured an interview for her, her family name definitely was a positive aspect of her ability to receive the position.

Subjects

The 10 women interviewed shared the common situation of employment in positions that involve leadership, supervision, and direction over their assigned employees. They also participated in decisions directly related to the organizations for which they worked. While all women were in a position that required them to direct others, four of the women were supervised by others and six did not report to a supervisors. Of the 10 women interviewed, four obtained their positions directly and four obtained their positions through family relations or the recommendation of others.

The participants had been in their current positions for at least two years. Most of the women assumed their current positions through previous related positions. Most leadership positions for women in Egypt are achieved through hard work, promotion, or by virtue of their relationships in family companies. The study's findings conclude that the participants between the ages of 25-38 generally obtained leadership positions on their own through promotions and job-related educational achievements. Women in the study over 40 generally held positions in their families companies with promotions based on family associations and patriarchal decisions made by the head of the company.

Participant 1. Participant 1 is 52 years old and has two children; a boy and a girl. The participant works at a private school in Cairo and has been a school administrator for five years. Her responsibilities include dealing with students, parents, dealing daily with parental concerns, teacher concerns and other issues related to the school. In addition, she helps the director and other administrators in solving problems related to the Egyptian culture and ways of life, primarily with foreigners not familiar with the community. She holds a degree as medical doctor but does not work in medicine. She stated, "I really did not have any interest in practicing medicine upon the completion of medical school, the income generated is not like in the US, one makes much less money and the work is time consuming."

She began working after she married and had her two children, a year and a half apart. She began working as a science teacher, as she has a background studying science and biology. She was interested in teaching because the time demands would be less than that of practicing medicine. At the time of seeking employment, the position was proposed to her by a friend of her sister's. She stated, "I was very nervous going to my interview I had never taught in a school before, my only experience was in training new nurses." In her previous jobs she had been consistently promoted by her superiors because she showed competence and a positive attitude.

All of the jobs she applied for in the past were due to her own effort and willingness to move forward. She obtained her present administrative position by being promoted in a previous job as a school doctor and science teacher to an administrative position. This of course gave her more relevant experience for her current position. The participant states, "I enjoyed my time in the classroom teaching science, but eventually I wanted not to be in the classroom anymore and this lead me to seek an administrative position."

In her current position, most of the other staff who she supervises are women as they all are in secretarial positions and office administration. There are only a few women occupying higher positions in administration; most of the administrators she works with are males. "It is common in this organization that men are in charge of the most important positions, positions at the top." As far as mentoring others, she has one female friend who is currently in one of the same positions she had prior to her move into administration. She tries to provide her with advice and help her as much as can through her prior lived experiences and support. The woman she mentors has a goal to advance and work in an institution of higher education, perhaps as a faculty member at a university, so Participant 1 is working with her in achieving this goal. "Many of the women I work with would like to obtain better positions, as secretarial work is not considered a difficult position and easy for woman."

Participant 2. Participant 2 is 35 years old and has two children, a boy and a girl. She works in a bank in a major city as the head of strategy and private banking. She has been in her current position for two years and has been working for 12 years in banking as a strategic finance manager and private banking manager. She has an MA and an MBA specializing in strategy and finance. When she applied for her current position, she did not have anyone, family or otherwise, to procure an interview for her or influence someone to interview her.

She is from a well-known family in the banking industry and this may have helped her to not only achieve the position but also open the door to gain knowledge in managing finances. She states, "In Egypt, family is a very important part of many aspects of life both in business and social status." Her family is known as a wealthy and successful family; both her mother and father come from families in the banking industry, and this influences what people think about her. People automatically make the assumption that she will be successful. She clarifies "I was very driven in school and worked fulltime while I was studying for my MBA, it was important to me to prove I had the skills required for money management." She concludes she was not hired just because of the family she came from, but a strong family name definitely helped in influencing employers.

Her MBA is specialized in strategy and finance, and this specific focus helped her to achieve the position she currently holds. There are four women in her section at the bank;

however, most positions at the bank are held by men. Approximately 25 of the people at the branch she works at are men. "Most banks in this region have predominantly men in the highest positions of the bank; there are exceptions, but not many."

Participant 2 is involved in a mentoring program that is part of a non-government organization (NGO) working on entrepreneurship goals with young women who want to start businesses. She provides them with business planning, management, and financial advice. She counsels them on preparing a balance sheet, marketing, budgeting, and planning their future as they try to start their own companies.

This participant is involved with the Young Women's Leadership Program (YWLP) in Egypt. This program offers opportunities for young women and training in professional and leadership skills, with the objective of empowering these young women to become involved and active in their communities. She says, "It is important for women to support other women in the decisions of their careers choices, and in influencing them to strive for prominent positions in any industry."

Participant 3. Participant 3 is 36 and has four boys. Currently, she is Head of Economics in a private educational institution and has occupied this position for two years. She has been working for this institution for 10 years. She has a PhD in economics and a Master's degree in education. Her doctoral work was in the field of business and economics, which pertains to the position she is in now. She states, "Most women outside of those working for their families in Egypt have procured jobs through their education and education level, it is an important aspect of employment for Egyptian women." In addition, she has been through intense training and other workshops that have enhanced her abilities and skills on the job.

There are only two other women at the same level of position she holds. She believes it is difficult for women to be in a position of this caliber. Her education, experience, and time at her institution all contributed to her current position. Again she states, "I must continue to go to workshops and trainings that relate to my position as competition for jobs like this is common." She mentors students, and one is a former student of hers. This former student is also a student advisor at school. Participant 3 advises her about her goals and what she needs to get into and successfully attend graduate school to further her career and education. The relationship between her and this particular mentee is very good. "I think I am a good role model for girls wanting to further their education as they see I have gone far with mine."

Participant 4. Participant 4 is 33 years old and has three children, two girls and one boy. She works for a well-known non-profit aid agency in Egypt and is a Director of Projects. She has been in her current position since 2003. Prior to working in her current position she worked for local NGOs and corporate foundations. She has a master's degree in Sociology and helps other NGOs to obtain projects that are generally in Egypt and focus on children and women. About her job she states, "Egypt has so many people who need help with everything from housing, food, education, and nutrition. Working with women and children is important to me. Although there are many NGOs in Egypt and worldwide, it is impossible to provide services to everyone."

She had no outside help from family or otherwise when acquiring her current position. She stated, "I decided long ago this is what I want to do, it is not a glamorous job and the pay is rather low. It is an acceptable position for women in Egypt. My husband works and this allows me to work in social services." Her education, previous jobs, and master's degree all assisted her in qualifying for her current position. She added, "Before I worked for NGOs, I did volunteer work. All of these things together have assisted me in obtaining this position."

Most of the employees in this particular sector of the work force, about 30 out of 40, are women. This is normal for this sector. "There are a few men as directors but they are in higher positions than women. For example, our CEO's, Project Directors, and Regional Directors are all men; this is also common among NGOs in Egypt."

In terms of mentoring, she works with and helps other NGOs to obtain projects, generally projects in Egypt, focusing on children and women. This assists not only the procurement of projects but also helps those in need. Again, she states, "There are so many people and families that need assistance that all NGOs thorough out the region are willing to help one another because the mission of this organization is to help as many people as possible."

Participant 5. Participant 5 is 46 years old and has a boy and two girls. She works for her family's company. The worldwide organization was established in 1975 and has more than 150 schools throughout the world. In 1980, the family company took over the organization and made it one of the top Arabic language schools in the city. Discussing her company she states, "The company began the first Arabic language school in the city in Egypt. Language schools are now very common but we try to be the best by offering programs for all ages and levels."

In this family business, Participant 5 is involved in the day- to-day management, attends major trade fairs, works with agents, and helps in business development in terms of marketing. She oversees IT additions, buildings and facilities, new products, and the construction of new residences for students attending the school. "Because there are many, many language schools in the city, I try very hard to make sure we have the best facilities. This takes a lot of hard work not only here in the city but internationally as well. I travel quite a bit because my children are grown and in school, I did not travel much when the children were younger."

Her current position directly correlates with all aspects of the company. Although there are other employees, the leadership roles in the company are occupied by family members. She says, "The company is so big and there are many uncles, aunts, and cousins working for the organization, it helps to keeps the quality of our programs. There has never been nor do we ever plan to have a person in one of the roles of leadership who is not a family member. Men dominate the highest positions of leadership in the company."

Although she does not mentor any women or girls per se, she does encourage her daughters to do well in school and learn as much as possible about the family business. "I encouraged both girls to pursue university and study in the field of business administration. I would like my girls to go into the family business, but I want them to concentrate on family and marriage as this is their first priority."

Participant 6. Participant 6 is 42 years old and has two boys and a girl. Currently she works in the family business, a big company. She has run her own section for the past seven years. The company has been in the family since 1925, but she established her section of the company as part of the group of family business. She stated, "My company is part of the larger corporation but I am the owner of this separate company within my families company, it is part of the group of companies in the corporation. This is ideal because having the family as support has definitely assisted me in the success of my individual business."

In the corporation, the highest positions are occupied by men as there are few women in the family who chose to work. She states, "There are two sides to working for family: there is pressure to be successful without the pressure of doing it on your own." Currently, there are no

women she is mentoring, as there are no women interested in employment at the firm.

Participant 7. Participant 7 is 47 years old and has three children, two girls and a boy.

She works in the family business with her father. The company has been in existence for 40

years. She began as a secretary, and then moved to the film department, the library, catalogue

department, the ordering department, and the furniture factory, where she learned Auto Cad,

produced programs, and became the manager of design. She adds, "I have always wanted to

work for my family's business, even as a young girl I would tell people I was going to work with

my father when I grew up." In addition to being the manager of design she, has been the vice

president for 18 years. She has a B.A. in business administration.

Participant 7 states, "Right now I am the only woman working for the company in what I

do, because it is small and not a multinational company. But many designers in the furniture

factory are women." In terms of mentoring others, she provides guidance to junior designers.

The company is well known as a place to learn about this type of business and many people use

it as a segue to opening their own business as an extension of the company. Of the company she

states," the type of work we do is a popular business in Cairo, and we like to help others get

started with their own companies as their company generally helps our company."

Participant 8. Participant 8 is a 37 year old and has two boys. She has been in her

current position for 10 years and took three years off to have her children. She is the head of

medicine in a private educational institution. Before that she worked in hospitals, and it took her

five years to complete her residency. Her family did not have anything to do with her career

choice and there are no doctors in her family. Consequently, the family did not assist in the procurement of both her career and position. "I am the only doctor in my family so I am encouraging my sisters to go into medicine. One is a dentist and the other is still in school."

Her education consists of a degree in family medicine and masters in pediatric medicine. The pediatric/family medicine aspect of her background enabled her to procure current position. She states, "It is very common for women doctors to be pediatricians, they are more accepted in the medical community. Other specialties continue to be dominated by men. You see very few women in medical positions other than pediatrics. On the other hand, you see very few men in pediatrics."

There are no women who hold a higher or equal position in her department, as she is the director of medicine at the school. She reports to the director and the owner; both are men. She has worked in different settings, including a hospital for individuals with mental retardation in Kuwait. She says of her background, "I think the combination of my different work experiences including my work with individuals with mental retardation was a big plus as the hospital was very well-known in Kuwait." She also contends, "The university I got my medical degree from is a very well-known institution in the United States and played a huge role in me obtaining this position."

Most of her mentoring is in the form of giving advice to students who want to go into the field of medicine. Many students ask what it takes to become a doctor. She is asked other questions like "Is it important to go abroad?"; "Does it take a lot of time out of your life?"; and "Is it a difficult profession?" Her mentees want to know about family life as well, and she recommends they choose a specialty that better fits the needs of their lives and family. She adds, "I am lucky as my children go to school here and it makes me feel safer knowing they are here if they need anything. They both started at the age of three and if I did not work at the school I do not think they would have started so early."

Participant 9. Participant 9 is 36 years old and has three children; two girls and a boy. She is head of pediatrics in a small practice. Prior to this job, she was a school doctor and before that, she took three years off for maternity leave. She began her career in a clinic and then spent three years in a hospital. She has a medical degree and Masters of Social Work in pediatrics. She has worked with people with handicaps and mental illness as well. She contends, "My work with people with mental and physical handicaps can often be like working with children. They have some of the same characteristics. For example, it may be hard for them to communicate and tell someone what is wrong or hurts." Her family did not influence her choices about working growing up. She wanted to be a doctor since she was very young.

Her family did not have anything to do with her career choice. She knows many people who have gotten jobs through their fathers, fathers' friends, colleagues, and faculty members without having prior experience, she adds, "This is especially true in petrol companies for both men and women. Petrol is a big business in Egypt and one of the professions that generally keeps only family members as employees. Granted, this includes extended family." No one in her family is a doctor or practices medicine. Having spent many years practicing in hospitals in pediatrics has helped her obtain the position she is in now.

She states, "I am the director, but all of the other doctors are women as well. Men do not go into pediatrics very often; it is seen as a woman's profession." There are no women in the practice who hold higher or equal positions. She supervises all of the doctors, and they are four women. Her supervisor is a man. She contends, "Although it would be nice to have my own clinic, it would make raising my children and taking care of my family difficult. I like that I do not have to worry about things like payroll, bills, and other thing associated with running your own practice."

She has encouraged three of her sisters to enter the medical field, whether it is medicine or dentistry. She supported her sisters with studying and passing exams in medicine and dentistry. Both of her younger sisters are dentists. She pushed her sisters to practice medicine instead of business. She feels like these professions are respected and in the pediatrics field usually women are preferred.

Participant 10. Participant 10 is 54 years old and has three boys. She works in her family's corporation. The corporation is one of the leading firms in human and goods transport in Egypt and works with many well-known companies in numerous fields. The family founded the company in 1936, and it is a leading Egyptian real estate development and construction company. Not only does this group work within Egypt, but also is increasing its presence in Libya, Algeria, and Saudi Arabia. She states, "The Middle East is in the midst of a huge building process and all over it seems there is new construction. Egypt's housing boom before the revolution was huge. It still is active but not as much as before." She adds, "The Emirates (Saudi Arabia, Dubai, and Abu Dubai) continue to build and prosper."

The company has over 10,000 employees and operates two other companies. As a leader in one of the first privately owned construction companies in Egypt, the participant is involved with every aspect of the business pertaining to advertisement and public relations. She likes what she does but admits, "It is mostly men who occupy the highest positions in the family business." Still, she says it is acceptable for a woman to hold her position in the company.

Findings and Conclusions

As stated previously, women in leadership roles in different cultures vary from country to country. The roles of women in Egypt reflects what men or society deem acceptable; these positions are generally in the areas of culture, family, women's issues, marriage, and education (Abu-Lughod, 2006). Exceptions, family ties and succession, pressure from social groups, pressure to appease the West, and commonly or usually appointed positions, play an integral part in the procurement of these positions occupied by women (Youssef, 2002).

Emergent Themes

The purpose of analyzing the data in this qualitative study was to attempt to identify emerging themes from the principal phenomenon (Creswell, 2002). "The clustered and labeled constituents are the core themes of the experience" (Moustakas, 1994, p. 121). The emergent themes were (a) family influence, (b) leadership position, (c) family obligations, and (d) level of education. Following the method as indicated by Moustakas, within each theme, "cluster[ing] the invariant constituents of the experience that are related into a thematic label" (p. 121) were completed to determine the themes. The identified themes were validated by reviewing the invariant constituents in connection with the emergent themes, according to the participants' verbatim responses to the interview questions (Moustakas). The following are the 4 emergent themes.

Family influence. Family and family life is very important in Egypt and considered a woman's first priority. Occupations that are amenable to this prevail in the women interviewed, doctors, teachers, administrators in schools, and NGO's were most common. Women generally are in charge of the household or other activities acceptable and appropriate by their culture. Most of the participants agreed that these occupations are frequently occupied by women. Of the 10 participants 5 (50%) obtained their positions without the aid of their family or other influences.

Working in the family business is a commonality as well. Often, it would be disrespectful to not go into a family business and do something else. One participant said, "It goes without saying you will work for your family if there is a successful business in place. I do not know of anyone in my circle of friends who has not gone into the family business." Most of the participants who worked for their families said that it would not even be an option not to go into the family business. Of the 10 participants 5 (50%) obtained their positions because of their family or other influences.

Working in a family business allows for women to continue to take care of their children, husbands, mothers, and extended family. Participant's indicated that the flexibility of working for their families enables them to fulfill what many of them called their "family obligation." One participant stated, "my husband and my children are really my first priority, making sure that they are ok and getting what they need is first and foremost. Between school, the club, the normal doings of a houschold, and work requires my attention 100% of the time. However, I do not successfully accomplish this without help" (assistants, drivers, and nannies for example).

One of the participants infers she is from a well-known family in the banking industry and this may have helped her to not only to achieve the position but open the door to gain knowledge in managing finances. She states, "In Egypt, family is a very important part of many aspects of life both in business and social status." Her family is known as a wealthy and successful family; both her mother and father come from families in the banking industry, and this influences what people think about her. People automatically make the assumption that she will be successful. She clarifies "I was very driven in school and worked fulltime while I was studying for my MBA, It was important to me to prove I had the skills required for money management." She concludes she was not hired just because of the family she came from, but a strong family name definitely helps in influencing employers.

Leadership position. The participants in this study were women in leadership positions in which they had been in their current positions for at least two years. Most of the women's current position was in direct relationship to previous positions that facilitated her achievement of obtaining this position. Leadership positions for women in Egypt are achieved either through hard work, based on promotion to higher positions, or positions in family companies. Expectations and social attitudes toward women continue to reinforce the perception both people have of women in Egypt.

Women have become a larger influence in the workforce; the cumulative contribution of women working in jobs that produce an income is increasing. Although all of the women expressed that yes, there are women who are leaders in management, guidance, and leadership there continues to be disconnect between leadership roles and women. One participant comments, "I do think there is change in the way women are seen in the workplace, but men are still seen as the driving force in most industries." In Egypt the predominance of values steeped in tradition continues to dominate men and women's belief systems and often are in favor of autocratic leadership.

The participants who worked for their family's companies generally were in leadership positions by default. The participants who worked for companies or organizations not of family relations mostly had leadership positions in the education, medicine, and NGO's. These women had all obtained their positions by applying, interviewing, and receiving positions without the aid of family or any other person known to them. One of the participants went through the normal application and interview process, however she reported that her families influence and reputation in the banking industry was definitely advantageous. She stated, "my reputation preceded me."

One of the participants who is a medical doctor talked about how many of her friends have families in the petroleum business. She stated that, "the petroleum business is probably one of the business in Egypt that has the most families working for one huge company, sometimes up to four generations of family members working together. In addition, these companies have been in business for 50-75 years, women in the family marry and often their husbands are employed by her family as well."

Family obligations. Unlike most cultures in the western world, women in Egyptian culture do not leave home until marriage and a career is very seldom put before a childrearing. One participant stated, "It goes without saying that women are generally expected to start having children very soon after they are married. Women in Egypt do not wait to start a family until after their jobs or careers, they have children and take care of their family first." This is not to say women do not work, they just have an obligation to family before work. One participant stated, "I became a medical doctor and immediately took three years before I started in a practice. I had my two children and as soon as they began school I went to work full time." Another participant said, "I wanted to get a job in a school where my children could go to school and I could be there with them. I was really lucky because I got a job at an excellent school where my children attend, I am still at the school and have been here since my children first started."

Many women have higher educations, MBA', PhD's, are doctors of medicine, doctors of dentistry, and university professors. The consensus from the participants is although they spend money and time on their educations, they often either wait a few years to work or do not work in the profession of training. One participant said, "Most women want to start a family right away after marriage, they will work if they want to after their children are old enough to go to school or nursery."

Family obligation influenced the decision of what kind of work, where to work, and when to work of the participants. One participant stated, "Although it would be nice to have my own clinic, it would make raising my children and taking care of my family difficult. I like that I do not have to worry about things like payroll, bills, and other thing associated with running your own practice." "It is very common for women doctors to be pediatricians; they are more accepted in the medical community. Other specialties continue to be dominated by men. You see very few women in medical positions other than pediatrics. On the other hand you see very few men in pediatrics."

Level of education. The 5 participants who obtained positions without the help of their families have advances degrees. Three of these participants hold medical degrees, one has a PhD, and 1 has a masters. One of the participants stated, "I really did not have any interest in practicing medicine upon the completion of medical school, the income generated is not like in the US, one makes much less money and the work is time consuming." The participants not working for their families procured jobs through their education and education level, it is an important aspect of employment for Egyptian women not working for their families. One of the participants expressed she felt it was important to encourage others to obtain higher educational degrees to improve their future employment opportunities, "I think I am a good role model for girls wanting to further their education as they see I have gone far with mine."

One of the participants worked as an NGO, She stated, "I decided long ago this is what I want to do, it is not a glamorous job and the pay is rather low. However, it is an acceptable position for women in Egypt. My husband works and this allows me to work in social services." Her education, previous jobs, and master's degree all assisted her in qualifying for her current position. She added, "Before I worked for NGOs, I did volunteer work. All of these things together have assisted me in obtaining this position."

Of the five women who worked for their families all held B.A.'s in various disciplines. One of the participants stated, I went to school and majored in a completely different discipline than business, which would have been advantageous to her families company, however this was not a requirement. She stated, "I have always wanted to work for my family's business, even as a young girl I would tell people I was going to work with my father when I grew up."

Summary of Findings

The participants in this study were women in leadership positions, which they had held for at least two years. For most of the women, their current positions were directly related to previous positions, which facilitated their advancement. Leadership positions for women in Egypt are achieved either through hard work, based on promotion, or because they were family members who are part of a family business. Women in the study between the ages of 25-38 generally obtained leadership positions on their own through promotions and achieving a higher level in education pertaining to their specific jobs. Women in the study over 40 generally held positions in their families companies with promotions based on family associations and patriarchal decisions made by the head of the company. In the study, all owners or heads of companies were men, either those who directly started the company or men who inherited their positions.

Family is a very important aspect of the Egyptian culture. A woman's first priority is getting married and starting a family. Family pressures, social pressures, and pressures from society continue to have influence on women in Egypt. Expectations and social attitudes toward women continue to reinforce the perception people have of women in Egypt. Women have become a larger influence in the workforce and the cumulative contribution of women working in jobs is increasing.

It is important to note that more women are now working. Egypt, like the rest of the world, is facing serious economic decline. It is often necessary for women to work for additional family income. Generally, the participants who had no family influence pertaining to job acquisition worked not only for the income generated, but also for benefits such as reduced or exempted school fees.

Chapter 5

Conclusions and Recommendations

The purpose of this phenomenological study was to investigate the perceptions and lived experiences of 10 Egyptian women emerging as leaders following the Arab Spring. This study applied a qualitative methodology to analyze the interviews of the participants' regarding their lived experiences. "Phenomenology (is) focused on the subjectivity of reality, continually pointing out the need to understand how humans view themselves and the world around them" (Willis, 2007, p. 53). As Moustakas (1994) explains, "Evidence from phenomenological research is derived from that person's reports of life experiences" (p. 84).

The aim of this phenomenological study consisted of applying the data accumulated from the interviews to a methodological analysis. Contained within chapter 1 is an interpretation of the implications of the data concerning the women and their importance in leadership. Chapter 2 contains a review of the literature encompassing a historical and theoretical perspective of women as leaders in Egypt. The research design and method is discussed in Chapter 3.

Included in chapter 5 is a discussion of the analysis for understanding the findings and discoveries presented in Chapter 4. The presentation and examination of the three themes that emerged from the responses of the interview questions from the participants' are also included in the chapter. Finally, Chapter 5 offers a summary of the data results presented in chapter 4, implication of findings and interpretation of the results of the data, results of research questions, significance of the study to Egyptian women in leadership, rumination on the study, recommendations, and a summary and conclusion.

Summary of Data Results

The literature in this study acknowledged that women leaders in Egypt have shed the conservative value system and joined the educated, professional communities. Nevertheless, discrimination, prejudice, domestic violence, restricted legal rights, lack of representation in leadership positions, and overall inequity remain (King, 2011). Women strive to continue in their pursuit of equality in all aspects of the current situation and cultural norms in Egypt. Religious and cultural traditions remain, dictating the appropriate and erroneous norms and behaviors expected of women in the Middle East (Thomas, 2011).

Changing the perceptions and oppressive attitudes of both Middle Eastern and other cultures have of women, Egyptian women continue to pursue their quest to become active in leadership positions through determination, perseverance, and desire to succeed (DeAnne, Cavanaugh,, & Sabbagh, 2011). However, a lack of research that addresses the issues Egyptian women currently face in their attainment of leadership positions persists. By acquiring an understanding of the lived experiences of a purposeful sample of Egyptian women attempting to find positions of leadership may benefit others in the future.

Themes

The study's results may offer evidence about prevailing cultural, political, and social influences and circumstances that women in the labor force experience. It is necessary for Egyptian women to recognize and discern the difficulty of establishing adjustments changes in the prospect of obtaining a leadership position within some organizations.

The collected data in Chapter 4 revealed four pertinent themes: (a) family influence, (b) leadership position, (c) family obligations, and (d) level of education. Egypt continues to experience a great deal of change politically, socially, culturally, religiously, and economically. One thing that has not changed is the cultural nuances that make Egypt a unique albeit challenging place for a foreigner to live. Egyptians are private people, and they socialize mainly with close friends and family. Bonds are strong among families and many work and live with their families, often within the same property yet in their own residence. Egyptians' privacy added a challenge to securing women for interviews.

Family influence. Family is one of the most important aspects of Egypt's culture. Most Egyptians consider the families well-being as the woman's first priority. Having and raising children, taking care of the household, anything pertaining to the function of the household, and attending to her husband's needs are the basis for this reality (Metcalfe, 2007). Half of the participants (50%) attained their positions on their own without the help from a family member or close relative. To procreate and produce children has always been a top priority and continues to be a part of Egyptian society and taken very seriously by all. This tradition continues in present-day Egypt (Hoodfar, 1997).

Many Egyptian men and women work for their families in companies and organizations. It is considered disrespectful to not work in the family business and hardly ever happens. Working in the family is a convenience for women as often they have flexibility and options in their schedule to attend to their family's needs. Recent studies have resulted in challenging the common belief that women are not capable of balancing their family obligations and management of companies (Cheng & Halpren 2010).

Leadership position. The participants in this study were women in leadership positions; however, social and culture norms pertaining to women support the perception about women as leaders in Egypt. It is common for many people to perceive a lack of women leaders in politics, private and public sectors, and judiciary positions (Kamal, 2011). Religion and culture continue to impose a set of acceptable behaviors and norms for women (Thomas, 2011). However, the uprisings in Egypt have resulted in more women emerging and engaging in leadership roles. Since the uprisings, the integration of women into leadership positions and their participation leadership roles have contributed to changes regarding women in the country (Guenena, n.d.).

Kamal (2011) investigated how women have risen as leaders in the Middle East, noting changes from the past and the present. It is indicated that there is now some equality and acceptance that allows women to share some of the responsibilities with men. The study observed a shift in the way men see women; they are dispelling their traditional views (Kamal, 2011). The study indicated that although minimal progress has been made, women are beginning to rise as leaders in Egypt.

Family obligations. Family in Egypt is considered the focal point of the social organization. The pressure of extending the family lineage results in the expectation to marry and produce children. The male figure is the dominant entity in the household and is accountable for providing all of the family's needs. The mother is the main person to care for the home, manage the household, and raise the children (Agathangelou, 2011). However, there are women who contribute their income to help support the family even though running the household is still their top priority (Metcalfe, 2007).

Half of the participants (50%) did not work for their families, most agreed their income helps and is needed because of the economic situation in Egypt. Two of the participants also noted that their positions in an educational institution helps in cutting the cost of tuition for their children.

Level of education. Of the 5 women who acquired positions on their own have advanced degrees. Three of these participants hold medical degrees, one has a PhD, and one has a masters. The study indicated that women not working for their families relied on their education and education level to obtain their desired position of employment.

More women in Egypt have faith in their qualifications and competencies necessary to hold leadership positions (Thomas, 2011). The study revealed that more women are attempting post-graduate degrees in their quest for better job opportunities. Education is seen as the catalyst for more women to be a significant factor in the fight for a better economy and life in Egypt (The Arab International Women's Forum, 2010).

Limitations

Limitations of this phenomenological study pertained to the conditions of (a) the size of the sample, (b) the participants visceral descriptions of their life experiences, (c) the exactness of the process of coding the information, and (d) and the data garnered from the interview. The sample size of 10 made it difficult to postulate and generalize reasons for obtaining positions of leadership. Sampling in phenomenological qualitative studies are limited to typically a sample of 6-10 intentionally and carefully chosen. Results cannot be applied to the general population (Creswell, 1994). Creswell's (1994) explained this limitation by emphasizing the objective of developing of comprehensive examination of a phenomenon, not arriving at a general application.

The second limitation is the participant's visceral descriptions of their life experiences. Leedy (1997) explains that the researcher forms a sense of "reality" of a subject or subjects' perceptions however he or she perceive it (p. 161). Essentially, this methodology examines a person or person's view of the experience as they see it (Altheide, & Johnson, 1994). The idiosyncratic make-up of qualitative investigations methods make the results difficult to apply to situations outside of the research (Polit & Beck, 2006).

The third limitation of the study is the exactness of the process of coding the information acquired from the participant's interviews. The coding process is characteristically prone to the researcher bias. For example, one's personal feelings about a subject may influence a researcher and the coding process. In addition, the researcher may bring information and theory from other domains and include them in the process of coding because they seem relevant to the data (Foss & Waters, 2003). The qualitative research process of researcher bias is recognized as unavoidable in research, therefore attention must be given to the data without grouping or connecting it to other disciplines theories (Foss & Waters).

The last limitation concerns the data garnered from the interview. Interviewers may be driven by their emotional, physical, and social situation. This would be the same as in the case of the person being interviewed. The researcher must consider this and listen to the interviews that were recorded. An evaluation of the tapes indicated there were no ambiguous replies based on the participant's mental and physical condition, and stress, anxiety of personal bias (Foss & Waters, 2003; Polit & Beck, 2006). Reactions from both the participant and the interviewer during the interview process had no bearing on interview data (Polit & Beck).

Many social scientists criticize qualitative research; frequently comments are made that it is simply a collection of narratives, personal feelings, and ideas effectively creating researcher bias in some situations (Berg, 2007).

Another criticism or contention placed on qualitative research is that there is an absence of the ability to replicate a study or research because it is impossible for another researcher to come to the same conclusions (Black, 1999). In addition, some are critical of qualitative research stating an absence the ability to formulate a concept inductively (Mays & Pope, 1995).

Recommendations

The significance of this phenomenological study pertains to women leaders and leadership in Egypt. The lived experiences of a selected sample of 10 women, all in positions of leadership in Egypt, were examined and analyzed to possibly shed light on the changes in leadership for women following the Arab Spring. The perspectives, opinions, perceptions, and insights were presented by these women pertaining to obtainment of positions of leadership in Egypt, a culture known for its a preference for men in positions of power and prestige (King, 2011).

In this study, the researcher obtained and utilized the participants' communications, expressions, and statements as the basis for exploring women in positions of leadership and the situations that led to their procurement of these positions. The purpose of employing the phenomenological methodology was to afford an innate perception of women in Egypt and the way they view the process of becoming leaders in the organizations or groups for which they work.

The methodology of this research disclosed the factors that currently are a reality in the lives of women in Egypt and their motivations and reasons for aspiring to be leaders in Egypt. The information gathered from this study may provide other women in Egypt with the opportunities to strive for positions that once may have seemed difficult. The research offers a view into the lives of women in Egypt working toward equality and independence and may serve as valuable information for the future women leaders of Egypt. It may offer a magnitude of possibilities for researching women and their quest to become leaders in a region of the world that often makes it difficult for women. Women from all around the world will benefit from the lives and experiences of these 10 women in Egypt.

Implications

Women aiming to advance their position face many obstacles; there are cultural attitudes, social, and legal dictums. This research offers women recommendations as how they may too move into leadership positions. It may offer some encouragement to women who aspire to occupy more significant roles through determination, perseverance, and desire to succeed (DeAnne, Cavanaugh, & Sabbagh, 2011).

This study provides information pertaining to the acquisition of leadership roles, offering motivation for women to seek leadership and showing how women acquired leadership positions in Egypt as it exists today. The participants in the study did take notice of that, prior to the uprisings in Cairo, women in leadership positions and women's groups were common. Nevertheless, opportunities have increase since the Arab Spring. Through a combination of structural issues related to economics, foreign policy, geography, demographics, the nation's political structure, and opposing factions for validity have formed the course of activism for women in Egypt (Thomas, 2011).

In Egypt, there are fewer leadership positions that the male dominated society deems appropriate and acceptable to women than men. Today women in Egypt may go to school, attend university, have employment in the civil sector, vote, and run for political office in elections. Women who show initiative may be swift to move into leadership positions, and the results of achieving goals established by these women are most likely realistic goals. What is more, the outcomes assist other women in their quest for leadership roles. Women as role models in Egypt are important for other women to witness, giving valuable information to other women and girls who aspire to be leaders. The significance of this phenomenological study pertains to women leaders and leadership in Egypt. The lived experiences of a selected sample of 10 women, all in positions of leadership in Egypt, were examined and analyzed to possibly shed light on the changes in leadership for women following the Arab Spring. The perspectives, opinions, perceptions, and insights were presented by these women pertaining to obtainment of positions of leadership in Egypt, a culture known for showing a preference for men in positions of power and prestige (King, 2011).

In this study, the researcher obtained and utilized the participants' communications, expressions, and statements pertinent to women in positions of leadership and the situations that led to their procurement of these positions. The purpose of employing the phenomenological methodology was to afford an innate perception of women in Egypt and the way they view the process of becoming leaders in the organizations in which they work. In addition, this study sought to understand the feelings and perceptions of these women and how they pursued their current positions of leadership. The methodology of this research disclosed the factors that currently are a reality in the lives of women in Egypt and their motivations and reasons for aspiring to be leaders in Egypt.

Recommendations for Research

The information gathered from this study may provide other women in Egypt with the opportunities to strive for positions that once may have seemed difficult. The research offers a view into the lives of women in Egypt working toward equality and independence and may serve as valuable information for the future women leaders of Egypt. Recommendations for further research entails observation of the current situation in Egypt. Close attention and analyses may yield a magnitude of possibilities for research pertinent to women and their quest to become leaders in the region of the world that often makes their aspirations difficult. Women from all around the world will benefit from the lives and experiences of these 10 women in Egypt.

As acknowledged in the literature, a significant gap exists in research that addresses the phenomena of women leaders in Egypt, The research in this subject is sparse and at the same time contradictory on some issues. This is the nature of the Arab culture because of the cultural norms pertaining to women. Even though there is some literature on the subject, data previously published indicates a need for more research on women as leaders in Egypt.

Recommendations for Leadership

By capturing the women's perceptions and lived experiences of emerging as leaders in Egypt, other women leaders as well as those who aspire to be leaders may benefit. They may learn more about leadership development of women, mentoring, and strategies in attaining leadership positions. This study was important to the area of research in understanding the connection between family, education, culture norms, gender, and attainment to leadership positions for Egyptian women.

The results of the study may provide evidence about prevailing family, social, cultural, occupational, and gender-related factors that affect Egyptian women in their quest for leadership positions. It is essential for both women and men in the region to recognize and comprehend the difficulty of establishing future changes for more women in leadership positions in not only the economic but the political arena as well.

Women in the Middle East and North Africa are increasingly accomplishing higher levels of education, becoming leaders of more organizations, and aspiring to political positions. Nevertheless, women continue to be under-represented in politics and leadership positions. Gender-biases, cultural restrictions, and societal norms are some of the barriers women continue to face in the post Arab Spring atmosphere. For women to become more involved in the political process, knowledge of current affairs and conditions are important prerequisites to raise social and political consciousness. It increases women's knowledge and advocacy efforts for not only women's issues but also current concerns.

Conclusion

Egypt since the Arab Spring has made many changes and yet some things have not changed at all. Political changes seemed imminent but now are dormant. There was a strong presence of women in protests, standing strong and proud. Unfortunately, the struggles and momentum represented by the young, liberal protestors who occupied Tahrir Square for days resulting in the downfall of the regime still have not translated into leadership roles. While the inner barricade of fear that women experienced was somewhat lightened post- revolution, the same cannot be said about their restriction of access to political roles. In parliaments following the Arab Spring, the representation of women has been deficient or nonexistent. In parliament, female representation consists of a mere two percent (Badran, 2011). The system of quotas was eradicated since the revolution and is a concern of certain women. However, other women are satisfied by this move.

The old regime and President Mubarak were ousted and anything relating to this group was dismissed. This included women who obtained positions by the quota system (*The Economist*, 2011). The standing of women in Egyptian politics has deteriorated significantly since the overthrow of Hosni Mubarak. "In the immediate aftermath of Mubarak's resignation, the SCAF announced the formation of a constitutional review committee to propose amendments to the constitution. The committee was composed of 8 men" (FIDH-World Wide Human Rights Movement, para 12).

The 1950s saw the development of women's groups and general civil society. However, these groups were repressed politically. Women's movements, specifically the women's rights movement originated in 1923 and founded by Hoda Shaararwi, were suppressed (Badran, 2011). Women of the elite, upper class were the leaders of this movement, nevertheless it was an autonomous, liberated effort by the civil society (Badran, 2011). The women's movement had many roles in obtaining women's rights. Some of these included a move to change laws pertaining to procedures, policies, and practices toward women. Women still do not share the same privileges as men in Egypt; discriminatory constitutions, biased mentalities, and unjust laws violate women's rights (Badran, 2011).

Gender-based violence continues to be an obstacle for women in Egypt. Women are not protected from spousal abuse and laws that safeguard them are for the most part absent in Egypt. In addition, the court does not see many cases of this criminal behavior. Sexual harassment is still an issue, and there were abominable incidents that women experienced in the protest. "During demonstrations, women protesters and observers were threatened, harassed and sexually assaulted. On the night of Mubarak's resignation, journalist Lara Logan was sexually assaulted by a mob of 40 men in Tahrir" (FIDH-World Wide Human Rights Movement, para. 7). Research from the UN indicates 99.3 percent of women in Egypt have experienced sexual harassment (El-Dabh, 2013). The research supports the expectation that harassment and assault happen regardless of the woman way a woman is dressed, how she appears, or how she conducts herself in public (El-Dabh, 2013).

There is however, an element of opposition concerning women's agendas, and it has grown more prevalent in the last year because of Islamist movements and the appointment of Mohamed Morrisy, who is in the Muslim brotherhood, as president elected after the Arab Spring (Kamal, 2011). After Mubarak was ousted, on "May 2011, SCAF issued a decree abolishing the

64 seat quota. Instead, the decree required all electoral lists to include at least one woman (Kamal, 2011). In practice, few women candidates were nominated and most of them were placed at the bottom of electoral lists. Women candidates won only nine seats in the 508-seat People's Assembly (upper house) and another 2 were appointed by SCAF, representing only 2%" (FIDH-World Wide Human Rights Movement, para. 7).

The Shura Council was formed in 1980 by way of an amendment in the constitution, directly following the revolution prior to Mohamed Morrisy (Marshall, 2011). In the 2012 elections, of the elected 180 elected seats, only four of were women (Marshall, 2011). The next president elected was to appoint 90 more (FIDH-World Wide Human Rights Movement, para. 7). The propagation of cultural morals supports conventional gender roles and principles, conveying these traditional norms and rationalizing the discrimination based on religion (Bandaran, 2011).

Following the Arab Spring, women's movements and women in the employment sector were positioned at the core of two extremely diverse but interconnected efforts (Thomas, 2011). Concurrently, from both these perspectives, women opposed the long-established patriarchal nature of social norms and governance of women in their societal groups and places of employment (Thomas, 2011). By functioning in a society traditionally dominated by men, women are beginning to proclaim their rights, at the same time braving their exclusion from politics and capitalizing on the way women are portrayed in the media by the West as victims of culturally ingrained oppression.

Many of the women who participated in the study expressed that women feel as if they are being heard. However, they are afraid that fear of increased crime, chaos, and economic disintegration will diminish their advance. Women working with NGOs question whether women are any better off following the revolutions. Women are still being harassed on the streets, seemingly now more than ever.

Egyptian women struggle to find their place in a male dominated political and social society. There is an intensification of the conservative nature of both society and political spectrums. Not only in Cairo, but also in more rural areas, women are reprimanded and even punished for how they are dressing. In addition, more women are choosing to wear the *niqab* (veil worn that completely covers the face, leaving a small space for the eyes to see).